Breed Lover's Guide™

GREAT DANE

A Practical Guide for the Great Dane

Janice Biniok

Great Dane

Project Team
Editor: Stephanie Fornino
Copy Editor: Joann Woy
Indexer: Elizabeth Walker
Design: Angela Stanford

T.F.H. Publications
President/CEO: Glen S. Axelrod
Executive Vice President: Mark E. Johnson
Publisher: Christopher T. Reggio
Production Manager: Kathy Bontz

T.F.H. Publications, Inc.
One TFH Plaza
Third and Union Avenues
Neptune City, NJ 07753

Printed and bound in China
11 12 13 14 15 16 1 3 5 7 9 8 6 4 2

Library of Congress Cataloging-in-Publication Data
Biniok, Janice.
  Great Dane / Janice Biniok.
      p. cm.
  Includes bibliographical references and index.
  ISBN 978-0-7938-4178-3 (alk. paper)
  1. Great Dane. I. Title.
  SF429.G7B56 2011
  636.73--dc22
                        2010003228

The Leader In Responsible Animal Care For Over 50 Years!®
www.tfh.com

Table of Contents

Chapter
1

History of the
Great Dane

The Great Dane is one of the largest dog breeds in the world, but his size is not the sole source of his greatness. He is great in dignity. He is great in heart. He is great in courage. He has so much greatness within his veins, in fact, that his image is larger than life. Some call him the "King of Dogs." He inspires so much respect, awe, and adoration from we mortals that he must surely have been a gift to humankind from the gods. His American breed standard even describes him as "the Apollo of dogs," as if he carries with him remnants of divinity.

Surprisingly, though, such a great dog did not descend from heaven. He traveled through the winding rivers of history, picking up the pieces of his greatness along the way. Occasionally, he scooped up a few odd colors or a rough coat from the canine gene pool. But he eventually emerged as the venerable creature we see today.

The History of Purebred Dogs

The concept of purebred dogs is a rather new development, historically speaking. Up until the late 1800s, dog fanciers bred their dogs according to type rather than breed. Although dogs of the same type shared many characteristics, such as size, structure, color, hair length, and temperament, these characteristics were not as defined and consistent as those possessed by dogs of modern breeds.

For reasons of practicality, people sought to produce dogs who could perform specific jobs, such as herding, hunting, guarding, or companionship. Some characteristics related to type were great assets in a dog's specific purpose, but other characteristics, like color, were highly prized for

The Great Dane is one of the largest dog breeds in the world.

their aesthetic appeal. Genetic mutations always gained much attention and sometimes became highly sought after.

Genetic experimentation was always ongoing, which is why all dogs, even purebreds, technically descended from mixed-breed dogs. As humans moved with their dogs into new territories, their dogs bred with local dogs, either through experimental or accidental mating. Historical events, such as the Roman conquests and the Industrial Revolution, fueled migrations of humans that contributed to the dispersion of different types of dogs throughout the European continent. Even dogs who had been geographically (and genetically) isolated from the rest of the world began to appear in different parts of the continent, thanks to improvements in travel, such as railway and better roads. Europe had become a simmering melting pot of canine DNA.

The Formation of Breed Clubs and Registries

It wasn't until dog shows became a popular and fashionable activity in Europe that dog fanciers became more interested in producing clearly recognizable breeds. This trend followed suit in the United States. Beginning in the mid-1800s, people began to enjoy showing off their favorite canines at loosely organized dog shows, and by the late 1800s, dog clubs devoted to specific

The Great Dane's immense size, graceful but strong build, and unique head profile appear in many ancient drawings and historical paintings.

breeds had started to form. These clubs drafted the first breed standards to document the ideal traits for their chosen breeds. Breed standards gave fanciers a roadmap to follow in producing dogs who shared identical characteristics.

Along with the production of breed standards, some dog clubs created studbooks to register dogs who met their breed's criteria for physical and temperamental traits. Eventually, it was necessary to form a national club to provide universal governance over registration and dog show events. Thus, the Kennel Club (KC) in Britain evolved in 1873, and the American Kennel Club (AKC) in America took root in 1884.

WHAT IS A BREED CLUB?

Breed clubs are local, regional, or national clubs formed by people who have a common interest in a particular breed. National breed clubs are responsible for establishing a breed standard, providing central governance over matters that affect that breed, and serving as the breed's representative with regard to purebred registry organizations. Regional and local breed clubs are usually members of a larger national club. They conduct activities at the local level, such as dog shows and training classes.

The Creation of Purebreds

By the early 1900s, most breed studbooks were closed, which meant that people could no longer register dogs who had unknown parentage, regardless of how well the dog matched the breed standard. In the interest of keeping bloodlines "pure," all dogs added to the registry from that point on had to be the offspring of dogs who were already registered. Breed clubs today rarely open their registries to allow the registration of outside dogs.

The Great Dane's Ancestors

Great Danes have carried with them several unique traits over the centuries that allow us to trace their lineage with a fair amount of confidence, even through the convolution of canine history. Their immense size, graceful but strong build, and unique head profile appear in many ancient drawings and historical paintings.

Early Ancestors

The earliest evidence of Dane-like dogs exists on Egyptian monuments and tombs. The tombs of Beni-Hassan, constructed between 2200 and 2000 BCE, contain many drawings of Egyptian dogs, and among them are depictions of large, strong dogs with short coats. These were most likely the forebears of the Molosser dogs, which were mastiff-type dogs who eventually gave rise to a number of large, powerful breeds.

Historians often trace Molossers to Asian war dogs used as far back as 1600 BCE. These dogs may have been precursors to the short-haired war dogs and hunting dogs who existed in ancient Persia around 500 BCE. Later, Molossers became a significant part of the Greco-Roman culture in the 1st and 2nd century BCE. Most commonly associated with massive Roman fighting dogs, these dogs were ferocious battle weapons and popular attractions in blood sports. Although heavier in build than our modern Great Danes, they certainly must have added a few genes to the "big dog" gene pool at the time. It's not surprising that an ancient Greek coin, called a Cunobeline, sported a likeness of a Dane-type dog.

Not all Molossers were of the broad-headed fighting dog type, however. Size, strength, boldness, and protective instinct were always defining characteristics, but large dogs came in different forms to perform different functions. A leaner build was favored for those used for herding and hunting. It was one of these leaner versions that may have contributed to the Great Dane's size and structure.

The Alaunt was a specific type of Molosser that some historians believe contributed significantly to the Great Dane's heritage. This was a short-haired, "light-bodied mastiff." This dog had common ancestral roots with other Molossers, but the Alani tribes that settled in the Sarmatian area north of the Black Sea are responsible for its development.

The Alani people developed several different strains of the Alaunt to meet their needs for hunting, herding, and war dogs. After the Huns conquered the Alani tribes

in the 4th century, Alaunts gradually found their way to other European countries. Their value as war dogs, protectors, hunters, and herders gave them a travel pass to just about anywhere on the continent. By the early 5th century, they had already found their way to France, Italy, Spain, England, and many other countries. The Alaunt name became so widespread in use by the Middle Ages that many Europeans used it to refer to a general type of dog, regardless of its background.

The Middle Ages

Interbreeding of dogs from different backgrounds was commonplace, and breeding records were practically nonexistent. Physical appearance and temperament were basically the only

The earliest evidence of Dane-like dogs exists on Egyptian monuments and tombs.

AGGRESSION IN THE GREAT DANE

Q: Does aggression still occur as a temperament problem in the Great Dane breed?

A: "Great Danes have been bred to have good temperaments for so long that aggression really isn't a problem anymore. If anything, Great Danes may be shy rather than tough."

—Randy Weaver, AKC judge and Great Dane breeder for 39 years

criteria people could use to judge a dog. Regardless of their potentially muddled ancestry, there is little doubt that some of the dogs identified as Alaunts during the Middle Ages were progenitors of the Great Dane.

The illustrations of Alaunts produced in Gaston de Fois' book, *Livre du Chasse,* in the mid-1400s, show dogs quite similar to modern Great Danes. Paintings produced during the medieval period also show dogs of excellent Dane type. The Great Danes in some of these works of art are depicted engaged in wild boar hunting alongside other types of boar-hunting dogs—a good indication that the Great Dane lineage crossed with other hunting and boarhound-type dogs. Specifically, the Old English Mastiff, the Greyhound, and the Irish Wolfhound are all suspected of contributing to the Great Dane's genetic makeup.

Boar hunting was a sport reserved for aristocrats. The Great Dane, being a large, high-maintenance animal, was not a very practical dog for farmers and peasants to keep. For this reason, you might consider the Great Dane to be a blue-blooded breed. Even today, Great Dane owners feel a sense of privilege in owning one. No wonder Great Danes think that they are entitled to lie on couches instead of dog beds!

The Great Dane's boar-hunting heritage also affected the breed's appearance. He no doubt acquired his hound-like ears from the hunting hounds in his ancestry. To prevent injury to such vulnerable ears, it was customary to crop the ears quite short. Today, cropped Great Danes possess much longer, gracefully cropped ears. Although cropping is now purely a cosmetic adaptation, some fanciers believe that it helps to preserve some of the breed's history.

The Great Dane's Name

It's clear that the Great Dane had become a well-defined and recognizable type of dog hundreds of years ago, but it's impossible to know exactly how he found his name. The breed obviously did not originate in

Denmark, although it had immigrated there, just as it had immigrated to so many other European countries. At some point, however, it became customary to refer to the breed as a Danish dog by use of terms such as "Danish Hound," "Large Danish Hunting Hound," "Danish Gallant," and "Grand Danois."

Historically, it was common to name animals after the places from which they came, regardless of whether that was the place of the animal's actual origin. In some cases, perhaps, people jumped to erroneous conclusions about the origin of some animals. Thus, we have guinea pigs that were never indigenous to New Guinea, and we have Great Danes that did not originate in Denmark. At some point in history, perhaps, breeders in Denmark exported some Great Danes to another part of Europe, and true to the customs at the time, people referred to these dogs as Great Danes. Eventually, the name came into common use for all Great Danes.

However the name came about, the Great Dane couldn't shake it. He acquired many other names over the centuries, including "Boarhound," "Ulmer Dog," "German Boar Hound," and "Tiger Dog," but the only name that had any staying power was "Great Dane."

When German breeders took a particular interest in developing the breed, between 1850 and 1890, they attempted to establish the name of

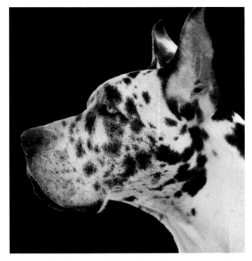

Despite the word "Dane" in the name, most consider the Great Dane to be a German dog.

"Deutsche Dogge," which means "German Mastiff," ultimately without success.

The Great Dane in Germany

Despite their failure to rename the Great Dane, the Germans still managed to make the breed "theirs." Most consider the Great Dane to be a German dog, as well they should. German breeders are responsible for improving the breed and strengthening its consistency in type. The breed became so firmly entrenched in Germany that it officially became its national dog in 1876.

German breeders initially produced different strains of Great Dane and called them by different names. These breeders unified in 1878, when a committee of breeders and judges decided to consider all varieties of Great Dane as the same breed. From this consolidation, common goals could be set to advance the breed, and German Great Dane fanciers subsequently drafted the first Great Dane breed standard in 1880. In 1888, German breeders formed the first Great Dane breed club, called the Deutsche Doggen Club.

The Great Dane In Britain

Some historians speculate that the Great Dane arrived in England prior to the Norman Conquest of the 11th century, but then the breed disappeared for a while.

These dogs would have been boar-hunting dogs. The disappearance of boar in the British Isles due to overhunting and shrinking habitat was possibly responsible for the breed's extinction in this area. But the breed was far too impressive to escape the notice of nobility.

In 1807, the Duchess of York imported a pair of Great Danes called Hannibal and Princess. Although described as "wild boar hounds," these dogs were definitely Great Danes. At that time, a variety of terms was still used to refer to Great Danes, but the Great Dane name had

The Great Dane Club of America was founded in 1889.

already come into quite common usage in some regions.

Great Danes began to appear at British dog shows by at least 1877. The KC added them to their Stud Book in 1884. And in 1953, a Great Dane finally achieved the highest honor—a Best in Show award at Britain's premier canine event, Crufts dog show. Champion Elch Elder of Ouborough, owned by W.G. Siggers, was the outstanding recipient.

The Great Dane in America

In America, the Great Dane's roots go back further than many other breeds in this relatively young country. Mr. Francis Butler imported the first Great Dane from London in 1857, well before dog shows became popular here. After German breeders focused their attention on improving the breed, many more fine-quality Great Danes were imported to America from Germany.

American Great Dane fanciers established the German Mastiff or Great Dane Club of America in 1889. Just two years later, the organization shortened its name to the Great Dane Club of America. After resolving the breed's temperament issues, American breeders found their own success in the show ring. They established their own lines of Great Danes, many using German bloodlines, and the quality of dogs produced was on par with those produced in Europe.

Americans not only accepted the Great Dane as a pride-worthy dog breed—they embraced the Great Dane as part of their culture. When Brad Anderson created the Marmaduke cartoon in 1954, he probably had no idea it would provide him with a lifelong career. As a Great Dane lover, you may find yourself collecting these cartoons, as they tend to embody the humorous spirit of Great Dane ownership. (Mr. Anderson gets many of his cartoon ideas directly from dog owners.) And who hasn't seen at least one episode of the Scooby-Doo cartoon series that has been a part of American television since 1969? Although lacking the courage of a real Great Dane, Scooby-Doo is just as lovable as the real thing.

The Great Dane's Reputation for Aggression

The Great Danes produced throughout history, even after the Germans had adopted the breed as their own, had quite sharp temperaments. Boldness and aggression were valuable traits for boar-hunting dogs, as boars were very dangerous animals to pursue. Two types of dogs were used in boar hunting: dogs who chased and cornered the boars, and dogs who attacked and held the boars so that humans could dispatch them. Great Danes, due to their size, strength and ferocity, fulfilled the latter duty.

Americans not only accepted the Great Dane as a pride-worthy dog breed but also embraced the breed as part of their culture.

While such a temperament might have been useful in boar hunting or protection work, it was not very practical in the show ring. Hugh Dalziel's book, *British Dogs*, published in 1879, mentions the notorious reputations of Satan and Proserpina, a pair of Great Danes owned by Mr. Frank Adcock. In dog show circles, these dogs became known as "the Devil and his wife."

British dog shows were not the only venue where Great Danes gave a negative impression. In 1881, Great Danes entered in a New York dog show started so many fights that the show superintendent banned the breed from future shows. The Great Dane's bad temper provided good cause to fear for the safety of exhibitors and their dogs. The breed did not participate in New York dog shows again until 1887.

And then, of course, there was probably a bit of pride and ego that went into producing dogs with the temperament of loaded guns. Before the start of the 20th century, Germany was already making a name for itself as a producer of fine protection dogs. German breeders staked their claim to a number of breeds used for this purpose, including the German Shepherd Dog, the Rottweiler, and the Doberman Pinscher. It only makes sense that the Great Dane, too, developed a fearsome reputation.

These episodes may have helped to shift Great Dane breeding in another direction. Maybe it was the decline of boar hunting that made such volatile temperaments in the Great Dane obsolete. Or maybe breeders began to realize the impracticality of producing giant dogs too dangerous to handle. Whatever the case, breeders worked hard to stabilize the Great Dane temperament, and their success was outstanding. In an amazingly short time, they had essentially purged the breed of aggression and replaced it with a temperament of friendliness.

Without sacrificing the Great Dane's protective instinct, breeders had created a people-loving dog who often gets along fabulously with children and other pets as well. By the early 1900s, the Great Dane had permanently hung up his bad boy reputation and become a family man. This new image suited him well and did wonders for his popularity. Today, it is rare to find a well-bred, well-trained, and well-socialized Great Dane with a bad streak.

TIMELINE

- **2500 BCE** — Drawings in Egyptian tombs show large, short-haired dogs similar to Great Danes.
- **1600 BCE** — Asian war dogs existed. These became progenitors of Molossers.
- **500 BCE** — Molossers were used by the Persian army as war dogs.
- **100 BCE** — Molossers were used by the Romans as war dogs, protectors, and herders.
- **300 CE** — The Alani tribes developed the Alaunt, a specific type of Molosser.
- **1400 CE** — Alaunts, or Great Danes, had spread throughout Europe by the Middle Ages. They were used primarily for boar hunting.
- **1800 CE** — German breeders began refining the Great Dane breed.
- **1857 CE** — The first Great Dane was imported to America.
- **1876 CE** — The Great Dane became the national dog of Germany.
- **1878 CE** — German breeders united to perfect the Great Dane breed.
- **1880 CE** — The first Great Dane breed standard was drafted in Germany.
- **1881 CE** — Great Danes were banned from New York dog shows.
- **1884 CE** — The Great Dane was added to the Kennel Club's Stud Book.
- **1888 CE** — The first Great Dane breed club, called Deutsche Dogge Club, was formed in Germany.
- **1889 CE** — The German Mastiff or Great Dane Club of America was formed. (The name was shortened two years later to the Great Dane Club of America.)
- **1953 CE** — Ch. Elch Elder of Ouborough became the first Great Dane to win Best in Show at Crufts dog show.

Chapter
2

Characteristics of the Great Dane

The Great Dane is a genetic masterpiece, a combination of physical and temperamental traits that complement each other with balance and symmetry. This breed is a bold work of art that is impressive to behold, but it requires the right environment. You wouldn't put a Picasso in an old farmhouse; nor should you put a Great Dane in surroundings that clash with his inherent qualities.

Physical Characteristics

The physical characteristics of the Great Dane are worthy of much admiration, and it's understandable that many people are attracted to the breed because of them. In fact, Great Danes tend to attract lots of attention no matter where they go! However, these traits offer advantages for some and disadvantages for others. Will you be able to enjoy all of the fabulous physical features of this marvelous breed, or will they be encumbrances for you?

Size and Structure

The "biggest" consideration, of course, is the Great Dane's formidable size. Males are a minimum of 30 inches (76 cm) tall at the shoulder and sometimes reach 36 inches (91cm) in height. Females are a minimum of 28 inches (71 cm) tall, but it's

The Great Dane will grow to be a large dog who takes up a considerable amount of space.

ENERGY LEVEL

You might be surprised to discover that your Great Dane puppy doesn't realize he's supposed to be a low-energy dog. Great Dane puppies have just as much rambunctious energy as any other type of puppy. They require just as much supervision, training, and socialization, too!

not unusual for them to reach 32 inches (81 cm) in height. Although this breed has graceful construction, with a sleek, deep-chested, Greyhound-like form, it is more substantial in structure than some of the willowy sighthounds. Thicker bones and heavier muscle give the Great Dane an agile but imposing presence. Males average 120 to 160 lbs (54 to 72 kg), while females average 100 to 130 lbs (45 to 59 kg). Occasionally, a Great Dane can tip the scales at close to 200 lbs (90 kg)!

Such a large size makes the Great Dane an interesting conversation piece for sure, but it also presents a few obstacles. His enormous bulk takes up a considerable amount of space. This means that more room is required for his giant-sized bed and for his eating areas. Even with adequate space for a Great Dane, it's not unusual for such a large dog to be "in the way" at every turn. Although the Great Dane has a reputation of being one of the few giant breeds that makes an appropriate apartment pet, space limitations suggest otherwise!

Size also impacts dogs in a not-too-favorable way. Large dogs typically are shorter lived than smaller dogs, with the Great Dane life span in the range of seven to ten years. You can expect your huge companion to come with huge expenses, too. A Great Dane can easily eat more than twice the amount of an average-sized dog. The cost of oversized collars, beds, feeding dishes, and other supplies puts the Great Dane at the top of the canine companion cost chart. You'll have to multiply the health care expenses for your behemoth buddy as well. A dog's weight often determines the cost of medications. Surgeries, including neutering and spaying, can also be considerably more expensive for giant breeds.

True Dane lovers are willing to make room to enjoy this fabulous breed, and they believe that the extra expenses are well worth the benefit of having more dog to love. But concessions aside, Great Dane owners must always be conscious of the enormity of their pets. Regardless of his

A Great Dane's ears can be either cropped or natural, like those pictured here.

however: They both possess a bold, regal posture.

The Great Dane's expressive eyes are usually dark colored. Light-colored eyes or eyes of different colors do occur, but they are not desirable for show dogs. Haws, which are droopy lower eyelids that expose some of the pink eye membranes, are serious faults in the Great Dane breed, as are Mongolian eyes, which give the Great Dane a somewhat squinty or small-eyed appearance.

Ears

One of the most notable features of the Great Dane's head is the ears. In America, where ear cropping is common in this breed, the sharply erect cropped ears are quite distinctive. They give the Great Dane an alert appearance and also show off the sleek undersweep of the breed's graceful neck. Unfortunately, this breed also seems to be prone more often than other cropped breeds to suffer slight imperfections in their cropped ears.

It's not unusual to see show dogs with curled ear tips or other minor defects, and while many factors can contribute to such undesirable results, Great Danes may be more at risk of such flaws because their ears are cropped to be so long and elegant. Although minor imperfections can have little effect on a show dog's career, be aware that cropped ears are not required to show a Great Dane. The

gentle nature, a Great Dane is a powerful dog with a lot of weight behind him. Cautions must be observed when this large dog is in the company of very small children or the elderly, as accidents can and do happen.

Head and Neck

The Great Dane's head, which sits atop a gracefully arched neck, has a high, dignified carriage. The male's head is broader and more masculine, while the female's is decidedly more delicate. The physical difference between the genders is quite obvious in this breed, not only in the size of the dogs but also in the strength or softness of their features. There is equality in one particular aspect,

The Great Dane's clean and easy-care coat is quite compatible with indoor living.

Great Dane breed standard allows for both cropped and natural ears.

The problem with attempting to show an uncropped Great Dane in America is that many breeders have not been breeding for the correct natural ear. But this should not be a concern for pet owners, who should weigh the pros and cons of ear cropping carefully before deciding to crop their dogs. In many cases, a breeder will already have her puppies cropped before they are ready for sale, thereby making the decision moot.

Body

The graceful curve of the Great Dane's neck leads into the smooth lines of his body. His chest is deep, and his tucked-up loins are an indication of his athleticism. The conformation of the Great Dane flows as gently as poetry and stands as firm as a rock. This makes the Great Dane both agile and strong. He is unique among the giant dog breeds in that he does not appear cumbersome or clumsy. Instead, he is quite nimble, despite his overbearing size.

His long, smooth tail descends to the hocks of his rear legs. Broad at the base and tapering to a fine tip, the tail is a powerful appendage that becomes whip-like when a Great Dane is excited. Without much density of fur to protect it, a Great Dane's tail is prone to injury if it strikes the corner of a wall, door frame, or other hard object. Once injured, it is resistant to healing and prone to reinjury. More than one Great Dane has had to have an injured tail amputated. This can be a career-ending situation for a show dog, as the Great Dane breed standard specifically disqualifies Great Danes with docked tails.

Coat

Although the Great Dane's size imposes demands on interior space, his fabulously

GREAT DANES AND RESCUE

Q: What is one of the most common reasons why people relinquish Great Danes to animal rescue organizations?

A: "People oftentimes do not realize how large a Great Dane puppy will be as an adult. They bring home a cute, cuddly puppy and before they know it, they have an unruly teenager. Without proper training, these dogs grow up without boundaries and can be a handful at more than 100 pounds (45.5 kg). Owners are overwhelmed and turn to rescue to take on their unruly Great Dane."

—Laura M. Rubin, Rocky Mountain Great Dane Rescue, Inc.

clean and easy-care coat is very compatible with indoor living. This short, close-fitting fur attire requires minimal grooming attention and doesn't collect mud or plant material to drag into the house. Great Danes, in general, are keen on cleanliness. Don't be surprised if you notice your Great Dane grooming his legs like a cat! Still, this breed is a moderate shedder, but you can minimize the hair in your home by brushing your Great Dane regularly, especially during shedding season in the spring and fall.

Although this short hair is a wonderful trait for a house pet, it also has some disadvantages. First, it doesn't offer the Great Dane much protection from the elements. This breed is not an outdoor dog. Second, it makes the Great Dane more prone to skin injuries. Contrary to the popular notion that Great Danes lie around all day and do nothing, this dog has plenty of spirit for play! Sometimes he plays a little too roughly and gets a bump or scrape. This is particularly common if a Great Dane plays with other dogs. Be prepared to treat minor skin abrasions when necessary. Third, Great Danes are prone to calluses when they spend too much time lying on hard surfaces. Most commonly, these hairless, thick-skinned patches appear on the elbows, hocks, and hips. Although they are generally harmless, they can become quite unsightly. They can also be permanent. If you have a lot of tile or hardwood floors, make sure that your Great Dane has soft bedding to lie on, both in his living quarters and his sleeping quarters.

Colors

One of the most delightful features of the Great Dane's practical wrapping is the colors in which it comes. The breed standard very specifically describes the patterns and markings of show Great Danes, but pet-quality dogs may show some variations. All of these color options are attractive in their own right and complement the other remarkable traits of this breed.

When choosing a pet, the color of your Great Dane rests largely on personal preference. But if you are interested in showing and breeding your Great Dane, great consideration should go into your color choice. Some colors, like harlequin, are more challenging to produce in show-quality dogs.

Brindle

Brindle, an eye-catching striped pattern, consists of a yellow-gold background color with an overlay of close-fitting black stripes. This pattern preferably includes a black mask over the face, and there may also be black on the ears and tail tip. Black eye rims and eyebrows give the brindle Great Dane a warm, intelligent appearance. Occasionally, a brindle Great Dane might have a small white patch on his chest or toes, but this is not desirable in a show dog.

Harlequin

Harlequin is another striking color pattern. This is basically a white dog with irregular, torn patches of black evenly distributed on the body. The contrast between the black and white colors is exceptionally powerful, which means that the harlequin definitely stands out in a crowd. The requirements for this color pattern are very strict in the breed standard, as a balance between the two colors is highly desired.

Fawn

Fawn, sometimes referred to as "tan," is probably the most common Great Dane color and the one most people associate with the breed. It consists of a deep yellow-gold color that covers the majority

The harlequin color pattern is quite striking on a Great Dane.

of the dog's body. Accentuating this attractive color are the black face mask, black eye rims, and black eyebrows. Black may also appear on the dog's ears and tail tip.

Blue and Black

There are two solid colors in the Great Dane breed: blue and black. The blue Great Dane is a rich steel blue color, and the black Great Dane is pure black. Both of these dark colors are exceptionally attractive in the Great Dane due to the breed's short, glossy coat.

Mantle

The mantle Great Dane, sometimes called a Boston, is a black dog with a white muzzle, neck, chest, legs, and tail tip. Often sporting a white blaze (stripe) on the forehead, this color pattern closely resembles that of the Boston Terrier.

Living With a Great Dane

It's important to consider the Great Dane's unusual size and strength when deciding to add him to your household, but his temperament is equally important. Believe it or not, humans and canines do occasionally run into personality conflicts. Powerful canine instincts can get in the way of a harmonious relationship. Conflicts can also arise if you are unable to meet the emotional and physical needs of a Great Dane. Can you get along with this type of dog?

Companionability

Great Danes have a lot of temperamental similarities, but they are also very individualistic. Companionability is one characteristic that features a wide range of possibilities. Some Great Danes are great with children and other animals, while other Great Danes harbor obvious dislikes. In either case, dogs who have become accustomed to children and other pets at a young age are more likely to tolerate them. Dogs who have not been raised with children or other pets need to be evaluated on an individual basis to determine if there will be any conflicts.

For the most part, the Great Dane's inherent friendliness tends to make him open to new relationships, but you should always take into account his enormous size. The Great Dane's "gentle giant" reputation is really quite misleading. It still hurts when this very large dog accidentally steps on you! In fact, a Great Dane's misplaced step can possibly break someone's toes. For this reason, Great Danes are not always a very good match for families with small children, elderly persons, or diminutive pets unless you are willing to take precautions to prevent accidents.

Still, there are many stories of success. A gentle Great Dane may adjust marvelously to a new baby in the home. Great Danes have forged unique friendships with dogs who are a fraction of their size, going so far as to crawl along on the floor to play with them. And many Great Danes get along famously with cats and other creatures that share their domiciles. There is rarely a cause to rehome a Great Dane because of changes to his living situation. This easygoing canine is exceptionally adaptable.

Drooling

One characteristic of the Great Dane that is not so attractive is his propensity for drooling. Big dogs have big salivary glands. These glands do not constantly overproduce saliva, but they do produce an amazing amount of saliva when they are stimulated. Don't be surprised if your Great Dane "springs a leak" and dribbles on the floor in anticipation of his dinner. Be prepared to clean up the inevitable splatters on walls, floors, and furniture. And you might want to make a habit of bringing a wipe rag along with you, just in case, when you are out and about with your Great Dane.

Environment

The Great Dane has been touted as one of the few giant breeds that can be kept in an apartment as easily as he can be kept on a sprawling estate. Although there are cases where Great Danes have indeed

Great Danes are not always a good match for diminutive pets unless you are willing to take precautions to prevent accidents.

become happy apartment dwellers, this is definitely not the ideal living situation for them (or their owners). Great Danes take up a lot of room. They leave massive stools to clean up. And unlike small dogs, who can get a good romp indoors, it's difficult for a Great Dane to get the proper exercise in an apartment situation.

Great Danes possess streamlined structures built for speed, and they do enjoy opportunities to open the throttle once in a while. Exercise doesn't have to consist of long or frequent runs. Sometimes just a single, short burst of running once a day is enough to satisfy them—one or two laps around the house.

GREAT DANES AND KIDS

For the most part, Great Danes live up to their reputation as "gentle giants" and get along fabulously with children, especially when they are raised with them. But a few precautions can minimize the chance of injury to children due to the Great Dane's substantial size:

- Make sure that your Great Dane cannot step on or bump into children when he is engaged in spirited exercise.
- Always supervise children around your Great Dane, and separate the dog from the children with door gates when you can't keep an eye on them.
- Teach children how to treat your dog appropriately, and don't allow children to crawl all over your Great Dane just because he tolerates it.
- Do not put children on your Great Dane's back, no matter how cute it looks. Great Danes are not horses, and you may injure your dog's back.
- Enlist children to help care for your Great Dane so that your dog can bond closely with them.

Apartment living usually isn't compatible with this.

Also keep in mind that Great Danes have difficulty negotiating small spaces. Their inflexible spines do not allow them to bend their long bodies sufficiently to turn around in very confined areas. Instead, they often have to "back out" of tight spots. A Dane is much more comfortable in an environment that is proportionate to his size.

An appropriate indoor environment is a particular concern for the Great Dane simply because he does not make a good outdoor pet. If a Great Dane proves too large for his indoor living space, it is not fair to relinquish him to a life of outdoor living. These dogs develop very strong bonds with their owners and can develop serious behavior issues when forced to live apart from those they love. The Great Dane prefers to be a somewhat pampered, highly valued member of the family. He is much too proud and stately to live in a doghouse!

Exercise

The common perception that Great Danes are "large, mellow dogs" is only half true. Great Danes reach a point in their maturity when they become rather lackadaisical. However, many owners have wondered when their dogs will finally reach that point! Great Danes are spirited dogs, and some of them are quite energetic even to the age of five or six years. It is during this period of life, when a Great Dane still has his rowdy spells, that he is most likely to injure himself, injure others, or break things. The best precaution is to make sure that your Great Dane has regular opportunities to exercise safely.

Overall, the Great Dane's exercise requirements are quite reasonable compared to other dogs. Even younger Great Danes who still have spurts of playful energy are easily satiated with a short game of fetch or tug. Even so, make

Great Danes are spirited dogs, and some are energetic even to the age of five or six years.

a point of interacting with your Great Dane as much as possible. The time you spend with your dog strengthens your bond with your big buddy and makes your dog more responsive to you. A daily walk is a wonderful routine to establish.

Independence

The Great Dane's personality can be as strong as his physique. He is an independent-minded dog, but this is not a fault. Although some people equate this type of canine mindset with stubbornness, it can be a very desirable trait. It is great for those who prefer a dog who is not overly demanding of attention. It is a perfect quality for a dog intended to be a trustworthy guardian of life and home, a job for which the Great Dane is well suited. And it comes packaged along with a trait that has endeared so many to this breed: devout loyalty.

In the Great Dane, loyalty is fierce. He is entirely devoted to the object of his adoration—his owner! He will do anything to please the object of his affection. He may even sulk if he feels that he has disappointed the one who owns his heart. But he reserves such esteem only for the person who is truly worthy of it.

To be worthy of a Great Dane's undying devotion, you need to be a firm, consistent, and trustworthy leader. Great Danes have little affinity for those who are overly heavy handed. They do not appreciate being manhandled or subjected to brute physical punishments. In fact, such treatment will put a Great Dane on the defensive and can make him quite mean and dangerous.

Likewise, Great Danes have little respect for those who are overly submissive and easily manipulated. Some are perfectly aware of their immense size, and they will push their weight around passive, tolerant humans. A Great Dane prefers an assertive, fair owner. A source of benevolent authority gives a Great Dane a tremendous sense of security, something that is profoundly important to him. The person who gives him this will gain a powerful canine ally. Without firm leadership, a Great Dane feels that it is his duty to take control.

Protective Yet Friendly

The Great Dane has a well-developed protective instinct, but it is not overbearing. While he initially prefers to "size up" a stranger upon first encounter, his naturally friendly personality quickly rises to the surface. Far removed from his vicious ancestors, the Great Dane possesses impeccable judgment in determining the difference between friends and foes. Those deemed to be friends can expect to be the recipients of his affection, which may include having a giant dog attempting to sit in their laps.

Great Danes love such physical contact. They have earned their reputation as "leaners" because they love to lean against people. You may need to enforce some boundaries with regard to this behavior because a "leaning" Great Dane can easily push someone over. But once a Great Dane decides that he likes someone, he often becomes a friend for life. Just as the Great Dane remembers those with whom he becomes smitten, he also has a long memory for those he doesn't trust. Those who breach the trust of a Great Dane can expect to be regarded with suspicion for quite a long time!

You must be firm, consistent, and trustworthy to win the Great Dane's respect.

Check It Out

CHARACTERISTICS CHECKLIST

✓ Evaluate your indoor and outdoor areas to be sure that you have room for a Great Dane.

✓ Prepare for the higher costs of food and health care for a large dog.

✓ Evaluate your own personality to see if you can get along with a Great Dane.

✓ Evaluate a Great Dane's individual personality characteristics to make sure that he is the right one for you.

✓ Consider the other people and animals in your household when choosing a Great Dane.

✓ Provide daily exercise for your Great Dane.

✓ Invest time in training your Great Dane.

Trainability

Of course, to truly enjoy walking your Great Dane, you'll have to teach him to walk nicely on a leash. A Great Dane who pulls can be downright deadly at the end of a leash. You'll have to teach your dog many other things as well because an untrained Great Dane can be a superior menace. His size alone makes him a danger to you and anyone else who comes in contact with him. And as for the Great Dane, his future is bleak if not totally dire if his behavior is uncontrollable.

Thank goodness Great Danes are relatively easy to train. They are of average intelligence when compared to other purebred canines, but they have a lot of "heart," which includes a strong desire to please and an honest work ethic. The thing that makes them especially receptive to training is the fact that most Great Danes are highly motivated by food rewards. Positive training methods work wonderfully for them!

But alas, you can spend a lifetime training a Great Dane without success if he does not respect or trust you. It can take time to earn a Great Dane's respect, especially if you have a particularly dominant dog or if you adopted an adult dog. Training classes can often help expedite this process. But when your Great Dane begins to relinquish his will in favor of yours, he'll do anything for you.

The Great Dane deserves every ounce of esteem he has earned from his many admirers. There is no other dog quite like him. When you make room for a Great Dane in your home and in your life, you'll discover there is only one word besides "great" to describe him—unforgettable.

Chapter
3

Preparing for Your
Great Dane

Welcoming a new dog into your life is an exciting start to a special relationship. This amazing creature will rely on you for all of his basic needs. Your Great Dane is like a child who grows very, very big and yet never grows up. Enjoy doting on your Great Dane buddy, as this is what makes pet ownership so much fun!

Pet Supplies

Preparing for your Great Dane doesn't have to be a serious task. Pet ownership has become so popular that myriad pet products have infiltrated the pet supply market. Going to the pet store these days can make you feel like a child in a candy store. It's fun to browse through all of the product choices, but always keep an eye out for practicality.

Bed

Dog beds are an absolute necessity for Great Danes. This is a very heavy dog. When he lies down, his weight causes his bones to put a significant amount of pressure against his skin. Because his skin receives little cushioning from his short, flat-lying coat, he can easily develop calluses or sores in bony areas such as the elbows, hocks, and hips if he spends too much time lying on hard surfaces. Your large lounger should have a bed anywhere he spends a lot of time lying down. This means that more than one bed may be required.

A dog bed is an absolute necessity for the Great Dane.

COLLAR SIZE

Check your puppy's collar frequently to make sure that it is not too tight. Great Dane puppies quickly outgrow their collars. You should be able to fit at least one or two fingers flat against your puppy's neck under the collar.

It's not always easy to find doggy beds big enough for such an enormous dog, and when you do find them, they can be quite expensive. Besides checking discount pet supply outlets, you might be able to find good deals from dog show vendors. And if all else fails, the most economical plan is to put two smaller dog beds together. In any case, always choose something that is durable and easy to wash.

Collar and Leash

When it comes to finding the perfect neckwear for your dog, keep in mind that wide, thick, or heavy collars can leave noticeable indentations in your Great Dane's sleek coat. Worse, they can chafe the fur off your dog's neck. A narrow but sturdy collar, like a rolled-type leather or nylon collar, may do the least amount of damage.

Those huge, black, pointy-studded collars might make your Great Dane look pretty cool, but they aren't very practical for everyday use. Go ahead and have some fun showing off your impressive dog with a fancy collar, but choose collars with safer flat studs instead of points, and take these collars off when the occasion is over.

Head halters are a newer option designed to deal with dogs who pull on the leash. Because these collars can put pressure on a dog's neck, they are not the best option for Great Danes. These dogs have long necks and a genetic tendency toward vertebrae instability.

The Great Dane requires a leather or nylon leash that is at least 1 inch (2.5 cm) wide.

Ask the Expert

FENCING

Q: Because most Great Danes are not fence jumpers, what size fence do they require?

A: "I recommend a 6-foot (2-m) fence simply because any dog kept behind a fence is more likely to become territorial, and you do not want a fence that people can reach over."

—Jolene Tikalsky, President of the Great Dane Club of Milwaukee and
Great Dane breeder for 30 years

This type of collar does not teach a dog to stop pulling, and its use is really unnecessary if you put sufficient effort into leash training your dog. Consult a professional trainer if necessary to find a training method that works for your individual canine.

Just like collars, leashes come in a variety of styles. The Great Dane requires a leather or nylon leash that is at least 1 inch (2.5 cm) wide. The most practical length is 6 feet (2 m), as this is the length most often required for dog training classes, and it works well for dog walking too.

Crates, Gates, and Ex-Pens

One of the things you will have to consider when you get a new dog or puppy is how you will confine your dog. Confinement is necessary to keep your dog safe, to assist with housetraining, to prevent household damage, and sometimes to separate pets at feeding time.

Crates

Crates have become a common method of confinement. But Great Danes are not common canines. A crate large enough for a full-grown Great Dane would be overbearing in any type of home. For this reason, many Great Dane owners opt for other methods of confinement. Even so, a smaller crate may come in handy for a Great Dane puppy, especially as a form of nighttime confinement or as an aid in housetraining. Adult-sized crates (for Great Danes, this means the largest size on the market) are generally only practical if you are involved in traveling with or showing your dog. In this case, a collapsible crate makes the most sense, as it won't take up as much room when it's not in use.

Gates

Door gates can provide a much easier way to restrict a Great Dane's household space. Most Great Danes are respectful of door gates, even though they look like they could easily jump them. However, if your Great Dane does prove to be a jumper, purchase an extra-tall model or double up your door gates by putting one on top of another. This way, you can confine your dog to a safe room when necessary.

Ex-Pens

Sometimes it's impossible to make a room completely safe, especially for a curious, naive puppy. Ex-pens (exercise pens) are great for puppy confinement because they can keep a puppy safe while providing enough room to play. Although an ex-pen does take up a considerable amount of room, it is only temporary, as your Great Dane puppy will soon outgrow it. Hopefully, you will have your puppy housetrained by that time, and he can graduate to having more freedom in the house.

Food and Water Bowls

Some suggestions are also in order for choosing food and water bowls. Plastic bowls are prone to chewing damage and can harbor bacteria when they get old. Crockery and porcelain may look nice, but it's best to avoid anything breakable. Stainless steel is often the best choice because it is durable and easy to keep clean. No matter what type of bowls you choose, make sure that they are dishwasher safe because you will need to wash your pet's bowls frequently.

There is some debate about whether raised bowls (bowls on a platform) are good or bad for Great Danes. On the one hand, raised bowls are supposed to help such a tall dog reach his food

Stainless steel food and water bowls are durable and easy to keep clean.

THE FIRST COUPLE OF WEEKS

It's not easy adjusting to a new home. Be patient with your Great Dane puppy as he acclimates to his new environment and routine. Sometimes puppies miss their mothers and littermates. If your puppy is prone to crying at night, try some of the following tips to help him sleep more soundly:

- Make sure that your Great Dane puppy gets some exercise at least an hour before bedtime to help him feel tired.
- Give him a light snack before bed to help him feel drowsy.
- Take him out for a potty break right before bed.
- Give him a warm water bottle wrapped in a towel to snuggle with.
- Make sure that his sleeping area is as comfortable as possible and that he has something soft to lie on. Chew toys may help him work off some stress so that he can sleep.
- A ticking clock, metronome, or soft music near his sleeping area may help calm him.

without ruining his posture or stance. On the other hand, raised bowls might encourage dogs to gulp air with their food, which can possibly contribute to bloat, a serious and often fatal condition. This may be a case where it is best to carefully consider your reasons for using raised bowls.

Unusually tall, leggy Great Danes may indeed find it more comfortable to eat from raised bowls, as did Gibson, a Great Dane who reigned as one of the tallest dogs on record. If you plan to show your dog, it is still customary to use raised bowls to help preserve a show dog's posture. There are, after all, many other precautions you can take to prevent bloat. But keep in mind that many Great Danes kept as pets do perfectly well eating at floor level.

Grooming Supplies

Although Great Danes are exceptionally clean dogs and their sleek coats rarely look disheveled, you should plan to obtain grooming supplies and establish a grooming routine as soon as possible. It is much easier to teach a Great Dane to tolerate grooming procedures when he's a puppy than to wrestle with him when he's an adult!

For hair care, you'll need a rubber curry brush to massage the skin and loosen dead hair and dandruff. Choose a curry brush that provides minimal coat penetration, as your Great Dane's coat is very short. A soft-bristled brush or chamois skin can provide finishing touches to your dog's smooth exterior.

Necessary hygiene items include a canine toothbrushing kit, large animal nail clippers, and ear cleanser. You should also purchase all of the bathing supplies you'll need. Your Great Dane will rarely require a bath, but you will never regret preparing for when he does. Dog shampoo, a spray nozzle, a squeegee (to remove water from the coat), and a large rubber mat for the tub are good things to put on your bathing supply list.

Identification

As a new pet parent, your primary duty is to keep your Great Dane safe. If your beloved pal gets lost, he won't be able to recite his name or home address to whoever finds him. This is why it's important to make sure that your dog carries identification with him wherever he goes. Most experts now recommend at least two forms of ID, the most popular of which are a collar with an identification tag and a microchip.

An identification tag is the first form of ID a person will look for on a lost dog. It provides instant information that can result in the speedy return of your pet. But because collars are removable or can slip off, a permanent microchip is the perfect backup plan. Most animal shelters and veterinarians now possess microchip scanners, and they use them routinely to identify lost dogs who come into their care.

It's just as important to obtain a license tag for your new canine companion as soon as possible. Most communities require dog owners to license their dogs, and they impose fines for noncompliance. While license tags do not reveal a dog's identifying information, they do provide a method by which to track down a lost dog's owner. They help a community keep track of its canine population and identify dogs that are up to date on rabies vaccinations. All of these functions are important for the safety of people and dogs alike.

Toys will provide your Dane with stress relief while he adjusts to his new home.

Toys and Treats

Toys may not seem like mandatory items, but they really are. Toys will provide your new dog with stress relief while he adjusts to his new home. They will give him an appropriate outlet for his chewing energy, and they'll provide opportunities for you to play with and bond with your new canine consort.

Dogs tend to have distinct preferences when it comes to toys. Your Great Dane might enjoy fetching balls or Frisbees. He might show a preference for tug toys. Your canine powerhouse might even surprise you by showing a fetish for soft, squeaky things. Start out with a small variety of toys, like Nylabones, to find out which types of toys your particular Great Dane likes, and observe him carefully to be sure that he plays with them appropriately. If he tends to tear toys apart and consume parts of them, restrict him to toys with heavy-duty construction.

One toy you might want to consider keeping in your arsenal of playthings is a treat-dispensing toy or a toy with a cavity that you can stuff with food. These are great for distracting or occupying your dog whenever the situation calls for it. You might also consider giving your dog a toy box for his things. He will appreciate knowing where to find his toys when he wants them, and he'll also learn to distinguish between his things and your things.

Treats are just as important as toys, as they are not just for spoiling your dog. If you want your new dog to develop good habits from the very beginning, treats will help encourage good behaviors. Most Great Danes are not very discriminatory regarding treats—they tend to think that all food is good food. Of course, that's not true. There is plenty of junk food on the market for dogs, just as there is for people. Avoid dog treats that contain sugar, artificial colors, or artificial preservatives. There are plenty of healthier alternatives, and your Great Dane will enjoy them just as much.

Preparing Your Home

Obtaining the supplies you need for dog keeping is only one of the preparations you'll have to make. Getting a new canine companion is a lot like starting a new job. You need to acquire the necessary tools to get the job done, but you also need to adjust your living situation and routines.

Indoor Preparations

This analogy is not too far-fetched: Caring for a Great Dane really is a part-time job. It pays to make this job as easy as possible. Always keep convenience and safety in mind when making the living arrangements for your giant friend.

Choose a feeding area that is easy to keep clean, as the Great Dane is notorious for dribbling water when he drinks. Decide on a sleeping area for your dog that will keep him out of drafts and allow you to keep an eye on him. Determine where you will keep your new dog when you can't supervise him. And identify any areas that need to be off-limits to your new pet, such as places where you keep hazardous or breakable items.

Your home is a completely new environment for your Great Dane. Your dog will probably be very curious and try to explore every object and every room corner, especially if he's a puppy. For this reason, it's important to check your home for potential safety problems. Exposed electrical cords should be covered or blocked off. Make sure that no small objects are lying around that could become choking hazards. And move

houseplants out of your pet's reach, as they may be toxic to your dog.

You'll have to observe your dog carefully for a few weeks to find out how he reacts to his new environment. Does he try to chew on the furniture? Does he like to play with the cords behind your electronics? Does he enjoy shredding newspaper all over the floor? Once you know if your Great Dane has any vices, you can adjust the environment or take corrective actions to prevent problems.

Your Great Dane needs a safe, appropriate outdoor area to play.

Check It Out

DOGGY PREP CHECKLIST

- ✓ Obtain at least two different forms of ID for your dog.
- ✓ Apply for a license for your dog as soon as possible.
- ✓ Keep practicality in mind when purchasing your dog's supplies.

- ✓ Decide where your dog will eat, sleep, and potty.
- ✓ Dogproof your home by checking for hazards.
- ✓ Check your dog's outdoor areas for safety, too.

Outdoor Preparations

You'll have to make sure that your dog's outdoor environment is just as hospitable for him as his indoor environment. Are there any dangerous areas that should be off-limits to your dog? Are there planted areas that you do not want your dog to disturb? Do you know if any of the plants are toxic to dogs? (Visit the ASPCA website at www.aspca.org for a list of toxic plants.) Enforce these off-limit areas as soon as you bring your dog home.

You'll also need to choose an outdoor potty area for your dog. This will help in housetraining your dog, as he will soon learn the purpose of this area and what he needs to do when you take him there. Once your dog becomes accustomed to using a particular area, it will be much easier to clean up after him. Let's face it: Great Danes produce big poops, and a yard can quickly become a doggy doo "mine field" with them.

Your Great Dane also needs a safe, appropriate outdoor area to play. This is

good for his physical and mental health. It is difficult for a Great Dane to stretch his legs in the house (without breaking something). But how will you confine your dog to your yard? A fenced yard is the ideal environment for most dogs, and there are many choices in fencing from which to choose—wood, wire, and chain link. Investigate the costs and feasibility of the various options.

If fencing is not practical in your situation, the next best thing is a trolley-type tie-out system that consists of a cable stretched between two buildings or trees. This will provide your dog with some room to run and play, and it is not as likely to result in worn patches of lawn as other types of tie-outs. Heavy-duty tie-outs appropriate for Great Danes are available, but precautions are in order for any type of tie-out.

Never leave your dog tied out without supervision, as there is always the risk that he will become entangled and strangle on the cable. It is also not advisable to leave your dog tied out for long periods. This practice, called "tethering," can increase a dog's aggressive tendencies. Hopefully, after you have sufficiently trained your dog in the *come* command and he has matured to the point of being the "homebody" that Great Danes tend to be, you will no longer require such a device to keep your dog in your own yard.

Dog Care Responsibilities

Your new dog-keeping job is a big one. Although it is common for one person in a household to bear the entire burden of dog care, there is more than one benefit to enlisting the help of others. In addition to spreading the workload, it gives the dog a chance to bond with other members of the household.

In the Great Dane's case, this can be especially important, as these dogs tend to form strong attachments to the people who care for them. This makes the Great Dane very inclined to become a one-person dog. Although this tendency can be an ego-booster for that one special person, there are distinct advantages to having a dog who learns to be responsive to other family members as well.

A Great Dane who doesn't respect or obey other household members can be difficult to control when his "one" person isn't around. He might get pushy or even aggressive toward other household members. He can also become overly dependent on his "one" person and develop separation anxiety or other behavioral problems.

It's perfectly acceptable and natural for a dog to develop an especially close relationship with his primary caretaker, but having other family members participate in his care will encourage him to regard them with a measure of respect too. Everyone, then, becomes a member of the dog's protected circle, or "pack."

So encourage others to take on some of the dog care duties, especially the hands-on activities like dog walking, training, grooming, and feeding. Even children can participate in chores that are age appropriate. Many dog training classes allow the whole family to participate. This way, everyone in your home can develop a special relationship with your Great Dane and become richer for the experience.

Preparing for your Great Dane isn't just about getting ready for your new dog; it's about embarking on a new lifestyle. This voyage will take you on an amazing trek to one of the most unique destinations in dog ownership. Your Great Dane will truly become one of the "biggest" things in your life!

Chapter
4

Feeding Your Great Dane

When it comes to caring for your Great Dane, nothing has a greater impact on your dog's health and well-being than his diet. More than likely, nothing creates quite as much confusion either. There are probably more choices in canine diet these days than there are dog breeds.

So how do you know which diets are healthy? How do you know which ones give you the most for your money? And how do you choose just one out of the host of choices available to you? You should not assume that any dog food that made it onto a supermarket shelf is adequate fare for a dog. We've learned much about canine nutritional needs over the last couple of decades, and it behooves any dog owner to become educated about the good, the bad, and the ugly in canine diets.

A Balanced Canine Diet

Dog foods that meet the Association of American Feed Control Officials (AAFCO) requirements as complete and balanced canine diets will have a statement printed clearly on the label: "Formulated to meet the AAFCO Dog Food Nutrient Profile." Although this indicates that a dog could certainly subsist on such a food, it does not guarantee quality.

Why is quality important? Quality in dog food is what gives your Great Dane his glistening, dandruff-free coat. Quality in dog food is what fuels your dog's energy and inspires his upbeat,

Quality dog food is what fuels your dog's energy and inspires his upbeat, happy attitude.

FOOD QUALITY AND BLOAT

Q: Does the quality or type of food (kibble, canned, raw, or home cooked) contribute to bloat?

A: "While some foods may make claims to prevent bloat, I have not seen any reliable data implicating or supporting the use of a particular diet to prevent bloat. Feeding a good-quality food is definitely important for growth and health, and there are many on the market in different forms."

—LeeAnne Sherrod, D.V.M., Mukwonago Animal Hospital, Mukwonago, WI

happy attitude. Quality in dog food is what keeps his internal organs working efficiently, especially his digestion. In other words, if you want a healthy, mentally sharp and physically attractive dog, you need to consider dog foods that go beyond the minimum requirements of "complete and balanced."

Evaluating Quality

A balanced diet needs to consist of certain components in certain quantities. But don't be too alarmed when you see long, complicated names on an ingredients list. Some of these items are vitamins and supplements that help to make the diet healthy for dogs. However, you should avoid foods that contain artificial additives. This pertains particularly to artificial colors, flavors, and preservatives.

Protein

For canines, the largest required dietary component is protein. Considered omnivores, canines eat both meat and plant material, with meat being the mainstay of the canine diet. Although a diet containing 18 percent crude protein is adequate for an adult canine maintenance diet, better-quality dog foods provide 22 to 24 percent. However, it's not just the amount of a crucial dietary component that indicates a food's quality; you also need to consider the source of that component.

Where does the protein come from? If it comes from a solid meat source like chicken, beef, venison, or duck, it comes from a quality protein source. Lower-quality sources of protein include meat by-products or meals, grains, or rice. So to fairly evaluate a commercial dog food, check two sources of information on the food label: the guaranteed analysis chart,

The right amount of fat in the diet contributes to your dog's healthy skin and coat condition.

which shows the percentage of necessary components, and the ingredient list, which shows the source of those components.

Because food manufacturers are required to list their ingredients in descending order by quantity, it's easy to determine the main source of protein in a canine diet—it will be the first ingredient on the list. But why does it matter where the protein comes from? The value of a food hinges partially on its digestibility and how much of it the body can actually utilize. Whatever the body can't use passes through the system undigested. In addition, poor-quality ingredients tend to have other undesirable characteristics, such as higher calories or unhealthy impurities.

Fat

Fat is another vital component of the canine diet. This is the second item listed on the guaranteed analysis chart for dog foods. This component provides energy and contributes to your dog's healthy skin and coat condition. A good-quality dog food will provide 12 to 14 percent crude fat from desirable sources such as chicken fat, flaxseed oil, or fish oil. Poor sources of fat include beef tallow and "animal fats," which are often the recycled waste products from restaurants and food manufacturers.

Carbohydrates

Carbohydrates are a great source of energy, but when it comes to commercially prepared canine diets, carbohydrates tend to be overdone. In an ideal world, a dog's diet would consist primarily of meat, but because meat is a very expensive ingredient, commercial dog foods contain plant sources of protein as well. Lower-quality dog foods may use wheat or other grains to meet a dog's protein requirements, but higher-quality foods will use better sources of plant protein, like brown rice and potatoes. Unfortunately, the best sources of plant protein also tend to be the highest in carbohydrates! Therefore, dogs can easily gain too much weight on a good-quality commercial diet.

For this reason, it's important to measure your dog's food and monitor his weight. Although there are a few canine diets available that provide higher levels of meat-based protein, they are beyond the budget of most pet owners and can certainly pinch the pocketbook of someone who owns a voracious Great Dane!

Vitamins and Minerals

Commercially prepared canine diets must be fortified with the appropriate vitamins and minerals to make them complete and balanced. Because of this, supplementing your dog's diet with additional vitamins is generally not necessary unless your dog's system is stressed by illness or pregnancy. Dietary supplements, too, are only necessary when a specific health condition warrants their use. Always seek the advice of your veterinarian before supplementing your dog's diet.

Preservatives

Prepackaged foods necessarily require some type of preservative, but better-quality dog foods typically use natural forms of preservative, such as vitamin E (sometimes listed as mixed tocopherols) or vitamin C. Avoid foods with artificial preservatives like butylated hydroxytoluene (BHT), butylated hydroxyanisole (BHA), or ethoxyquin. The impact of such chemicals on canine health is questionable.

Dogs require a high level of protein in their diets, and the best source of protein is meat.

EOSINOPHILIC PANOSTEITIS

Great Dane puppies can sometimes experience a growth disorder called eosinophilic panosteitis. This is a painful condition characterized by inflammation around the bones. Your veterinarian can recommend diet options that can help minimize symptoms until your puppy outgrows this.

Cost Comparisons

Even though Great Danes have a slow metabolism and often require less food per pound (kg) of weight than smaller dogs, they can still consume considerably more food than an average-sized dog. So, how much more are you going to have to spend to feed a big dog a good-quality diet? Realistically, most good-quality dog foods cost about the same as lower-quality dog foods, and here's why: Lower-quality dog foods often contain fillers, like corn and beet pulp, which pass through the dog's system undigested. Because of this, it takes a greater quantity of low-quality food to maintain a dog's weight.

For instance, you may need to feed your Great Dane five or six cups of a lower-quality commercial dog food per day to maintain his weight, whereas you would only need to feed your dog three cups per day of a quality food. Good-quality foods cost more per pound (kg), but they tend to last a lot longer than the cheap stuff. Hauling tons and tons of dog food into the house to feed a big dog—envision scenes from the movies *Beethoven* or *Turner & Hooch*—is funny in the movies but not in real life. Also, keep in mind that the more dog food your dog eats, the more yard cleanup you'll have to do!

Even good-quality commercial dog foods are not perfect. Dogs require a high level of protein in their diets, and the best source of protein is meat. Unfortunately, meat is a very costly ingredient, and even quality dog food producers tend to use some plant sources of protein to keep their prices affordable. Dog foods that provide the highest levels of meat-based protein, including commercially prepared raw food diets, are considerably more expensive. These types of foods tend to bruise the wallet, especially when it comes to feeding a large dog like the Great Dane, but they are the most natural and healthy types of canine diets available.

When choosing to feed one of these pricey alternatives, also consider the potential savings in veterinary costs. A quality diet is the best preventive in health care. And then there are those benefits that money just can't buy—the pride in owning a dog who looks as healthy as he feels and the extra years of memories you're able to collect as a result of your dog's greater longevity.

Commercial Dog Foods

Commercially prepared dog foods come in different qualities, but they also come in different forms: dry, canned, and semi-moist. If you choose to feed a commercially packaged dog food, dry kibble should be the primary component of your dog's diet. This is the most economical form of commercial dog food because it has more nutrition packed into it, by weight, than any other.

Dry Food

Dry dog foods (kibble) come in an abundance of choices, including those that are appropriate for different life stages or energy needs. Specialized diets are also available to help manage obesity, food allergies, or other health conditions, some of which are available only through veterinary prescription.

There is sure to be a dry form of dog food that meets your particular dog's nutritional requirements. But because dry dog foods contain very little moisture,

it's even more important than usual to provide your dog with plenty of fresh water when feeding this type of diet.

Canned Food

Canned foods can be just as nutritionally complete as dry foods, but because they contain up to 90 percent water, they actually provide much less food by volume. It would take many cans of dog food per day to satiate a Great Dane! However, canned foods are by far the type of commercial food most preferred by dogs. And no wonder—they're so soft and flavorful! Although it wouldn't be economically practical to feed your

A nutritious diet will help keep your dog happy and healthy.

PACKAGING FOR PROFITS

Product packaging is a good medium for advertising. Don't be fooled by attractive packaging or savvy marketing ploys. The use of words such as "premium" or "gourmet" has no bearing on the quality of a pet food. According to the U.S. Food and Drug Administration (FDA), "Products labeled as premium or gourmet are not required to contain any different or higher quality ingredients, nor are they held up to any higher nutritional standards than are any other complete and balanced products." In addition, the term "natural" has little significance. The FDA warns that this term does not have an official definition, and it is not synonymous with "organic."

Great Dane canned food alone, your dog will certainly appreciate a little bit of succulent canned cuisine to supplement his dry fare.

Semi-Moist Food

Semi-moist foods are those that are soft but not as wet as canned foods. These often come in pouches or cellophane wrappers, and they sometimes look like artificial hamburger patties. These foods usually contain artificial preservatives and unhealthy flavor enhancers like salt and sugar. While this type of food probably isn't harmful in small amounts, it is not a good option as a regular diet choice. If you're not sure if a food falls under the semi-moist category, check the ingredients list and evaluate the food for quality. Most semi-moist foods will fail the quality test.

Non-Commercial Foods

Commercially prepared dog foods are convenient and economical, but they do have their drawbacks. There are concerns that some of the nutritive quality of commercially prepared dog foods is lost during the high-heat manufacturing process. In addition, it's not always possible to accurately evaluate the quality of ingredients. Food labels do not reveal if the ingredients are of a quality fit for human consumption or if they were unsuitable for human consumption. (If they are not suitable for humans, how can they be healthy for dogs?)

There is also the problem of trust. In 2007, hundreds of pets died as a result of melamine poisoning linked to tainted pet food ingredients. In 2006, Diamond Pet Foods had to recall 50 varieties of its food due to contamination with aflatoxin, a toxin produced by mold. It's not surprising that pet owners are taking a greater interest in what their pets are eating. Such awareness has inspired many pet owners to seek noncommercial diet alternatives for their precious furry friends. Both home-cooked diets and raw food diets have become quite popular.

Home-Cooked Diet

There's no doubt that home-cooked diets are made of human-grade food, as pet owners obtain the ingredients directly from the grocery store. These ingredients may include cooked meats, eggs, vegetables, and cottage cheese—items that could very well be salvaged from the dinner table. But don't be fooled. There is a big difference between feeding your dog table scraps and feeding him a home-cooked diet.

You must measure the ingredients of a home-cooked diet to create a balanced diet for your dog. In addition, supplements and vitamins are required to make the diet complete. In other words, you have to manufacture your own "complete and balanced" dog food, and this can be a somewhat time-consuming endeavor. However, you can minimize preparation time by preparing several days worth of food at one time.

If you are interested in pursuing this diet option, it is important to learn as much as you can about canine nutrition and consult your vet as well for some pointers.

Bones and Raw Food (BARF) Diet

Perhaps the most popular alternative diet is the bones and raw food (BARF) diet. This diet is perhaps the most natural diet you can provide for your dog. It doesn't come with the "baggage" associated with most commercially prepared or home-cooked diets. There is no heating process to leach nutrients out of the food. And thanks to its popularity, pet food manufacturers now offer a commercially packaged version of a raw food diet, which eliminates most of the preparation time.

The commercial version of the BARF diet comes in frozen patties that are easy to thaw as needed. Because commercial raw food already contains the appropriate vitamins and supplements for a complete and balanced canine diet, it is almost as convenient as any other type of commercially prepared dog food. Once sold only through dealers, it has now become widely available through many pet supply outlets.

Alas, even the BARF diet, regardless of whether it is commercially produced or home prepared, isn't without flaws. It is almost impossible to replicate all of the qualities of real "prey" for our predator

Maintaining a regular feeding schedule is good for both your dog's mental and physical health.

pets. Raw diets often lack the fibrous tissues of a fresh kill, which would help to "floss" our pets' teeth clean. It also may not contain the internal organs of prey, which might provide other natural and essential nutrients. Safety is another concern, as raw food requires proper handling to prevent the growth of bacteria.

The best practice when considering any type of alternative diet is to do plenty of research and consult your vet before taking on the responsibility of formulating your own dog food.

Healthy Feeding Practices

A nutritious diet alone isn't enough to keep your Great Dane healthy. You have to engage in healthy feeding practices, too. You can put the best quality ingredients into your dog's fare, but it can still make him fat. You can spend hundreds of dollars feeding your dog the best diet available, but he can still develop behavioral problems related to improper feeding practices. You can invest ten hours per week home-cooking your dog's meals, and he may still develop a life-threatening case of bloat. If you care enough about your Great Dane to give him the best-quality diet you can afford, make sure that you know how to feed it to him!

Feeding Schedule

Maintaining a regular feeding schedule isn't just good for your dog's physical health; it's also good for his mental health. Dogs like to know what to expect. They thrive on routine—it gives them a tremendous sense of security. A dog who can count on being fed at regular times each day will be less anxious and therefore, less susceptible to developing behavior issues like destructiveness or excessive barking.

In addition, a regular feeding schedule helps regulate your dog's entire system. It encourages regular elimination habits, which makes it easier to predict when your dog will need to go outside. It influences his patterns of activity, which makes it easier to meet his exercise requirements. And it helps establish good nighttime sleeping habits.

So feed your dog at the same times each day. For your Great Dane, this means at least two daily feedings—one in the morning and one in the evening. Once-a-day feedings can contribute to

bloat, an extremely dangerous condition in which the stomach becomes overly engorged with food and gas. For this reason, it's safer to feed a Great Dane smaller amounts more frequently, rather than large amounts all at once.

When your dog has had ample opportunity to eat his meal (about 20 minutes), remove any uneaten food until the next feeding. The practice of "free feeding," which involves allowing a dog unrestricted, free access to food at all times, will negate all of the

Regular exercise will help keep your Great Dane from becoming obese.

Check It Out

FEEDING CHECKLIST

✓ Evaluate the quality of ingredients in commercial dog foods.

✓ Choose foods with natural preservatives.

✓ Do plenty of research before implementing a noncommercial diet.

✓ Keep your dog on a regular feeding schedule.

✓ Feed your Great Dane at least twice per day to prevent bloat.

✓ Remove any uneaten food until the next feeding time.

✓ Measure your dog's food.

✓ Check your dog's weight occasionally, and adjust the amount you feed him when necessary.

✓ Limit the amount of treats and edible chew products your dog consumes.

benefits of having your dog on a regular feeding schedule. Although free feeding is one of the best ways to create a corpulent canine, it can also result in an underweight dog due to the lack of a regular eating schedule.

Measuring Food and Monitoring Weight

Dogs are scavengers by nature, and that means that they are very opportunistic when it comes to eating. If there is food, they will eat it—and they won't necessarily stop eating when they're full. Wild canines never know when their next meal will be forthcoming, so they tend to gorge themselves when food is available to store up as many calories as possible. Your Great Dane, too, may be predisposed to overeat when given the chance, but fortunately, he has you to

monitor his intake. You should take this responsibility very seriously and measure your dog's food.

When you know exactly how much your dog is consuming, it is easy to adjust his diet if he begins to look a little too thin or a little too heavy. The problem is that weight gain or loss tends to occur so gradually that it can easily escape your notice. This is why it is important to make a conscious effort to look at your dog's condition occasionally.

Does his body appear to be rounding out into a barrel-like shape? Conversely, are his ribs sticking out? If you suspect that your Great Dane isn't at his ideal weight, feel his ribs. A dog in good condition will have a light layer of fat over his ribs. If it is difficult or impossible to feel your dog's ribs, he probably needs to go on a doggy diet. If his ribs are exceptionally easy to feel, you might need to increase his food.

Obesity

When you are diligent about monitoring your Great Dane's weight, it's possible to catch weight problems early and correct them with simple diet adjustments. But managing your Great Dane's weight requires much more than this. Obesity has become a common problem for pets, just as it has for people. To prevent your Great Dane from joining the swelling ranks of pudgy pooches, make sure to give your dog an opportunity for a healthy lifestyle.

Some of the greatest obstacles to a healthy weight include:

Meal enhancements. It is best not to get in the habit of enhancing your dog's meals with people food. Not only can this create a finicky eater, but it adds unnecessary calories to your dog's diet. Even the best-quality canine diet will become unbalanced and unhealthy with the addition of meal enhancements. If you need to add something to your dog's meals to stimulate his appetite, choose a healthy canned food instead.

Too many treats. Treats are great for rewarding your dog for good behavior, but you should always limit your dog's treat consumption. Do not give your dog treats just to spoil him; spoil your dog with lots of time and attention instead. (He'll appreciate it just as much.) When using treats for training, limit the amount you use and adjust your dog's meals to compensate for his treat consumption.

Consumable chew products. Certainly, dogs need things to chew, but limit the amount of consumable chew products you give your dog. Rawhides, pig's ears, and even food-stuffed toys all add to your dog's calorie intake.

Lack of exercise. Dogs, like people, seem to be gravitating toward a more sedentary lifestyle. Great Danes, more so than most other dogs, are often content to reconcile themselves to such a life of leisure, but this doesn't mean that they don't need or enjoy regular exercise. Make sure that your dog gets a daily walk, at minimum.

Dog diets have come a long way in the last century, from table scraps to gourmet dog foods. We've learned much about canine nutrition, and we continue to learn more. Every stride toward better health for our pets gives us happier dogs to enjoy!

Chapter
5

Grooming
Your Great Dane

Your Great Dane comes with one of the cleanest, low-maintenance coats in the dog world. Although he is a moderate shedder, he does not collect the dirt or mats that curly-haired or long-haired breeds tend to collect. He does not have a thick, fluffy undercoat that tends to cling to every piece of furniture and clothing. In this sense, the Great Dane is truly both beautiful and practical.

You might think that this wash-and-wear kind of dog doesn't require much grooming attention, but you'd only be partially right. Although Great Danes do not require intensive care for their coats, it is still a healthy practice to brush them once a week. They require nail clipping just as often as any other dog. And they require just as much dental care, ear care, and eye care as other dogs. So don't neglect to give your giant beauty the care he deserves!

The Benefits of Grooming

Caring for your Great Dane's hygiene is as important to your dog's health as feeding him the right food. Grooming can help prevent physical problems for your dog. Regular nail clippings prevent foot, leg, and back problems. Ear cleaning can prevent ear infections. Dental care prevents periodontal disease.

Grooming can also help you detect health problems early and treat them before they become more serious. Did you find any fleas in your dog's coat? Did you notice any lumps? Did you find any patches of hair loss? Does your dog react sensitively to an area you touched?

Grooming your dog is obviously a good investment in your dog's health, but it is much, much more than that! It is an important bonding activity. As you touch and handle your dog's various body parts in the process of grooming, your dog gains confidence and trust in you. Other people may also benefit from this trust. Your veterinarian will certainly appreciate examining a dog who doesn't mind having his feet or ears handled!

Grooming is a good investment in your dog's health, but it's also an important bonding activity.

Puppy Love

INTRODUCTION TO GROOMING

Introduce your Great Dane puppy to the grooming process slowly. Keep grooming sessions short, but be sure to handle your dog's ears, mouth, feet, and tail. This will help desensitize your puppy to having his body parts touched. Try to work with your puppy when he is tired rather than when he is bubbling with energy, as he will be more cooperative. Teaching your dog to tolerate grooming is valuable education that will benefit your dog throughout his lifetime.

As if these benefits weren't enough, grooming has very practical advantages as well. Every time you remove the dog hair from your dog's brushes, you can remind yourself that you will have that much less hair lying about your house. Your well-groomed dog will get a lot more attention, too, as people enjoy petting a dog who doesn't leave gobs of shed hair in their hands. He'll be easier to live with and more appealing to your guests. But above all, he'll be an attractive dog of whom you can be very proud.

Coat Care

Coat care for your Great Dane actually begins before you groom him. Diet is a major contributor to your dog's healthy skin and coat condition, so if your dog has a dull coat or seems to be suffering from a chronic case of dandruff or excessive shedding, first make sure that you are feeding him a good-quality diet. If these conditions persist despite a good diet,

consult your veterinarian to rule out a medical cause.

Brushing

Your Great Dane grooming kit should include a rubber curry brush. This item should provide minimal coat penetration because your Great Dane's coat is quite short. Anything with long nibs or very coarse ridges is going to irritate your dog's skin.

How to Brush

Use this brush in a circular, massaging motion over your dog's entire body. This helps loosen dead hair, stimulate the skin, and bring dandruff to the surface of the coat. (Do not use the curry brush on your Great Dane's extremities. Your dog has extremely short hair on his head, legs, and tail, which makes them sensitive to abrasive brushing. Use only very soft brushes on these areas.)

Next, use a soft-bristled brush to smooth out the coat. Brush the coat in the direction it normally lies. Take your time with this, and let your dog delight in a few long, relaxing brush strokes. Grooming is one of the best ways to show your dog how much you love him!

Afterward, use a chamois skin or soft hand towel to wipe down the coat from the head toward the tail to distribute the natural oils evenly. This will give your dapper Dane a fabulous shine. If you thought that your dog looked just fine before you groomed him, this will definitely convince you that grooming does indeed have an impact on your dog's appearance.

Scheduled grooming sessions will help keep your Great Dane looking his best.

Bathing

It can be quite a chore to bathe a jumbo-sized dog, but the Great Dane has a couple things going for him. First, he doesn't require a bath very often. And second, his short, close-fitting attire rinses easily and dries quickly. The only obstacle, really, is his size.

With the right equipment, you can bathe your dog in the tub. A large rubber mat is required to prevent slipping and to protect your tub from those giant doggy nails. If you don't have a handheld shower attachment, get a spray nozzle to attach to your shower pipe or water spout. Some people find it easier (although messier) to wash their Great Danes in a laundry room or utility room that has a water source and a drain in the floor. Others decide to forego the challenges altogether and take their big buddies to a professional groomer.

It is a good idea to think about how you will handle bathing your Great Dane before a situation arises that requires your dog to have a bath. Great Danes sometimes play with skunks or roll in stinky stuff, just like any other dogs. If you decide to bathe your dog, keep a few tips keep in mind. Unless you have specific needs, the best type of dog shampoo to use is a mild, tearless shampoo. Never use human shampoos on your dog, as they are much too harsh. Also, assemble all of your bathing supplies before getting your dog wet. Your tub mat, spray nozzle,

Ask the Expert

SHOW DOG GROOMING

Q: What kind of specialized grooming does a show Great Dane require?

A: "They need to have their whiskers shaved to give them a cleaner, smooth look. We use color shampoos, and we use a Dremel tool to file their nails back quite short. This gives them a nice high stance on their feet. We start when the puppies are ten weeks old and trim their nails every two weeks, which pushes the quick back."

—Jolene Tikalsky, President of the Great Dane Club of Milwaukee and
Great Dane breeder for 30 years.

shampoo, towels, cotton balls (to keep water out of your dog's ears), squeegee (to remove excess water from the coat), and leash should be set up within arm's reach in the washing area.

How to Bathe

When you get your dog wet, start with the feet first and work your way up the legs to the body. This gives your dog a chance to adjust to the water, which should be warm but not hot. It's a good idea to finish washing his body before you get his head wet because once your dog's head gets wet, he'll want to shake. It is better to have him shake at the end of the bath rather than throughout the bathing process!

Avoid getting water in your dog's ears or shampoo in his eyes (even if you are using a tearless shampoo). When rinsing the head, it sometimes helps to hold your dog's nose down and shield it with your hand so that water doesn't run into his nostrils.

After you have thoroughly shampooed and rinsed your dog, use a squeegee on his body to remove excess water. This will help minimize drying time. A thorough towel drying is all that is required for a Great Dane. You can soft-brush his coat to smooth it out and then let him air-dry. You might want to put towels on his dog bed until he is completely dry, but don't let him outside to dry. He's sure to roll in the dirt and grass! And it can be especially dangerous to your Great Dane's health to let him outside during frigid weather while he is still wet.

Nail Care

Does the thought of clipping your dog's nails make you nervous? When you learn how to do it properly, you'll discover that there's really nothing to be nervous about. There are many different types of pet nail clippers on the market these days. You can choose whichever style suits you the best, but just make sure that it is heavy duty and can handle trimming your Great Dane's monster-sized nails.

How to Trim the Nails

The first step is to teach your Great Dane to tolerate having his feet handled. It's impossible to clip a Great Dane's nails if he doesn't want you to do it. Handle your dog's feet regularly, and if he shows any tolerance whatsoever, reward him. You can also do "mock" nail clippings that involve going through

The Great Dane's short, close-fitting coat rinses easily and dries quickly.

the motions without actually clipping the nails. When you do this, always do things the same way and in the same order. Your dog will become confident with this procedure if he knows what to expect.

Once your dog has gained confidence, the next step is to gain a little confidence for yourself. The reason that so many people are apprehensive about this care duty is because they fear clipping the nails too short. Cutting into the "quick," which is the nail's blood supply, can cause pain and bleeding for the dog. However, precautions can help prevent this.

If your dog has light-colored nails, the quick may be visible as a dark center within the nail. If you cannot see the quick because your dog has dark-colored nails, you may be

able to tell how much of the nail is excess growth by looking at the nail from the side. If not, you can cut or file a little bit of the nail at a time, always keeping in mind that it's better to leave the nails a little long rather than cut them too short. You can tell if you are getting close to the quick if you see a small dot appear in the center of the nail's cut surface. This is a clear indication to stop cutting. If you are inexperienced at nail clipping, it is a good idea to keep styptic powder or another blood coagulant product on hand "just in case." After you've completed a few successful nail trims, you may just get a "feel" for doing it.

If nail clipping still makes you nervous, you can always try a "foolproof"-type nail clipper. Some battery-operated models grind down the nails a little at a time or use a laser beam to detect the quick. And if all else fails, you can pay a professional groomer to take care of this chore. In any case, there is no reason to neglect your dog's nails. Overgrown nails affect the conformation of the foot and can cause foot, leg, and even back pain for your dog.

Ear Care

Inspect your Great Dane's ears regularly, whether they are natural or cropped. Some Great Dane fanciers believe that natural ears are more prone to ear infections because of the lack of airflow under the ear flaps. Moisture trapped within the ear canal then becomes a

Choose whichever style of nail clipper suits you and your dog's nails best.

breeding ground for bacteria. But the truth is that all Great Danes, regardless of how they wear their ears, have very deep ear canals that provide an ideal habitat for the proliferation of bacteria.

How to Care for the Ears

Symptoms of an ear infection include red, cracked, or crusty skin on the underside of the ear, ear odor, head tilting, and ear scratching. If you think that your dog has an ear infection, have him examined by your veterinarian. Treatment may consist of antibiotic ear ointment.

Ear infections can be very painful and irritating. It is in your dog's best interest to be proactive in preventing them. Part of your weekly grooming routine should include cleaning your dog's ears with an ear cleanser. For Great Danes with floppy ears, a cleanser that contains a drying agent, like alcohol, might be the most beneficial. Your veterinarian is the best person to recommend an appropriate product for your particular dog.

Eye Care

Great Danes do not typically develop unsightly tearstains as some breeds of dog do. They do not have long hair that can grow into the eyes and scratch the corneas. Nor are they prone to eye injuries, as are dogs who have protruding eyes. Even so, the sense of vision is so vital to a dog's quality of life that it is

Check It Out

GROOMING CHECKLIST

✓ Brush your Great Dane weekly.
✓ Check your dog for injuries and signs of illness while grooming.
✓ Trim your dog's nails every three to four weeks.
✓ Clean your dog's ears weekly to help prevent ear infections.

✓ Treat any kind of eye injury as an emergency.
✓ Brush your dog's teeth at least once per week.

important to pay attention to your Great Dane's eyes.

How to Care for the Eyes

If your dog's eyes appear red, swollen, teary, squinty, or cloudy, take him to the vet immediately. Eye injuries are always an emergency. In many situations, once vision is lost it is not always possible to restore it.

Protect your dog's eyes by applying an ophthalmic ointment prior to bathing your dog. (Even tearless shampoos can sometimes be irritating.) Shield your dog's eyes with a towel or cloth when applying insecticides to him. And do not allow your Great Dane to hang his head outside the window of a moving vehicle, no matter how much he loves to do it. Airborne debris can do a significant amount of damage to the eye, especially when traveling at car speeds.

Dental Care

Most domesticated dogs do not benefit from the dental-friendly diet of their wild cousins. Dogs on a commercial diet do not have the opportunity to gnaw on bones and tear at raw muscle tissue, actions that would help to keep their teeth clean. Instead, they chew on hard kibble that breaks apart before it can scrape the teeth clean. Your Great Dane may actually do more gulping than chewing anyway, thereby bypassing any dental benefits his food might provide. Soft dog foods are even worse, as they tend to stick to the teeth and create plaque and tartar, which can accumulate along the gum line and eventually cause periodontal disease.

How to Care for the Teeth

When the American Veterinary Dental Society (AVDS) declared that 80 percent of dogs show some degree of dental disease by the age of three years, it became quite clear that canine dental care is a necessity, not an option. The good news is that the Great Dane is not as prone to dental problems as small dogs. Great Danes can be heavy chewers, so it's easy to meet some of their dental needs by supplying various forms of dental chews.

Still, you'll want to inspect and brush your Great Dane's teeth at least once a week. Although smaller dogs routinely receive veterinary teeth cleaning under anesthesia, this is not a good procedure for Great Danes unless they require specific dental work. Giant dogs are much more likely to suffer complications from anesthesia, and it is not a good idea to subject your dog to anesthetic procedures unless absolutely necessary. It is a much better plan to keep your Great Dane's teeth in good shape from the beginning.

When handled properly, your Great Dane may even look forward to having his teeth brushed. It won't matter so much to him whether you use a canine toothbrush, finger applicator, or dental wipes, so choose the one with which you feel the most comfortable. Your dog will be most concerned with the flavor of toothpaste. Purchase an appropriate canine toothpaste in one of the many doggy-delectable flavors, such as beef or liver. You might want to try a couple different flavors or brands to find one that really excites your dog.

Start out by brushing only his front teeth, and leave him asking for more. Each week, you can add a few more teeth to this routine until you can brush all of your dog's

teeth. Most importantly, follow up each toothbrushing session with a very special treat—preferably a dental product, like a Nylabone, that will provide an excellent finishing touch to your dog's dental care. With so much to look forward to, your dog will be begging to have his teeth cleaned!

One of the greatest joys of Great Dane ownership is the pride such a dog gives his owner. Great Danes are impressive and imposing. But grooming your Dane gives you an active role in making your dog much more than that. A well-turned-out Great Dane is canine beauty on the grandest scale!

If you start good grooming practices when your dog is a puppy, he will more readily accept being groomed as an adult.

Chapter
6

Training Your
Great Dane

It's exciting to enter the wonderful world of Great Danes. Your Great Dane, likewise, probably thinks that it's pretty cool to enter the wonderful world of humans. In order to cohabitate successfully, humans and dogs have to find a way to "meet in the middle." You have to make concessions in your lifestyle to own a dog, and your dog needs to learn how to conduct himself properly to fit in with humans. It's not always easy to combine dog culture with human culture, but training helps bridge the gap.

Why Train Your Great Dane?

Owning an untrained dog is like owning a beautiful house without a roof or a sports car without an engine. An untrained dog is nice to look at, but not very practical and certainly not much fun. When it comes to Great Danes, an untrained dog can even be dangerous. Remember, this dog is the size of a small pony! He is very strong and very determined to have his own way.

Almost every Great Dane has the potential to become someone's dream dog. But not one of them is born a perfect pet. Until you educate him, your dog only knows how to act like a dog. Dogs bark and dig. They jump up to greet people. They chew on things and soil the carpet. For these reasons, training is not an option—it's a necessity.

In addition to learning how to be a good member of your household, your dog needs to learn how to be a good member of society. Neighbors will not be very happy to have their neighborhood terrorized by a Great Dane! In this sense, an untrained Great Dane is a tremendous liability to his owner. It is much cheaper to invest in training than to pay lawsuits instigated by a delinquent Dane. There are many good reasons to educate your dog, but the greatest may be the fact that training builds a very strong bond. It fosters trust and respect. When you learn to communicate with your dog through training, you may discover a special

When it comes to Great Danes, an untrained dog can be dangerous due to his large size.

connection that makes you feel as if you can read your dog's mind. Your Great Dane can become more than a pet—he can literally become your soul dog.

Positive Training Methods

There are many different ways to teach a dog any particular skill, and this is a good thing. A technique that works for one dog may not be so successful with another. It helps to have options available when you run into a roadblock in training. However, it's very important to use only positive training methods when teaching obedience skills.

Positive training methods involve the use of rewards to encourage the repetition of good behaviors. You'll need to ignore incorrect behaviors. You should never use punishments when teaching your dog new skills. If you snap your dog's leash every time he doesn't respond exactly the way you'd like, he will eventually stop trying to learn. To your dog, it's like attending a school where the teacher hits you on the head every time you get a math question wrong. Pretty soon, you stop trying to answer the questions. If you keep your dog motivated by providing rewards for correct responses, he'll keep trying to earn those rewards.

Any training technique that requires you to hit or otherwise physically harm your dog is not a training technique—it's just cruel treatment. It undermines your dog's trust in you. Great Danes are not

Training will build a strong bond between you and your dog.

very receptive to violent training methods. Unlike more submissive breeds that may tolerate such abuse, Great Danes have a strong self-preservation instinct. They are more likely to defend themselves and develop problems with aggression if they are ill-treated.

There really is no reason to treat your noble friend so callously. Your Great Dane longs to please you. You will go much further by nurturing his will to please and enlisting his willing cooperation. Then you'll know that your dog is obeying from the heart, not out of fear.

Canine Leadership

A Great Dane who adores his owner will do anything asked of him. But to gain

DEVELOPMENT AND LEARNING

Young dogs go through various developmental stages that influence their learning. Be aware of the following mental growth stages that affect your dog:

0 WEEKS– 8 WEEKS	Puppy learns important canine social skills from his mother and littermates. For this reason, puppies should not be removed from their mothers prior to the age of eight weeks old.
8 WEEKS— 12 WEEKS	Puppy may develop a fear of unfamiliar things. This is also a "fear imprint" stage, when bad experiences can result in very strong fears. It is important to socialize your puppy at this stage and make sure that his introduction to new stimuli is positive. The puppy can benefit from some obedience instruction at this age, but his attention span is short and much repetition is required. This is a good time to begin housetraining and crate training.
12 WEEKS— 6 MONTHS	Socialization is still very important at this age, but the puppy begins to develop some independence and a desire to explore. His attention span is getting longer, and his retention is getting better.
6 MONTHS— 2 YEARS	This age period is often referred to as a dog's "teenage years." Young dogs often become somewhat belligerent as they test their limits to see where they fit within the social hierarchy. This developmental stage requires a lot of patience, but it is also a great time to seriously pursue obedience training, as the dog is very receptive to learning at this age.
2 YEARS +	Dogs slowly transition from juveniles to adults at this age. Concentration and focus become much stronger, and this is a good time to pursue more advanced training goals.

your Great Dane's adoration, he must first respect you. If you ever want to be able to control your Great Dane's behavior, you have to be on a higher rung on the social ladder than your dog.

Many conflicting messages are circulating within the dog training community these days regarding the "alpha dog" concept. Some behaviorists have gone to great lengths attempting to debunk the "alpha dog myth," but don't take this the wrong way. This does not mean that we should be on an equal status with our dogs. Dogs are genetically programmed to find their place within a social hierarchy, regardless of whether that hierarchy consists of humans or other dogs. In some breeds, like the Great Dane, this programming is stronger than it is in other breeds.

The alpha dog debunkers are really trying to discredit the common perception people have about the alpha dog role. People tend to think that, in order to be in control, they must dominate by force or coercion. Isn't that what real alpha dogs do? Don't they bite, fight, and snarl their way to the top of the canine social ladder? The answer is no, they don't. Fighting is actually more common among dogs who don't know where they fit within the social structure. Alpha dogs already know where they belong—at the top.

In this sense, being a canine leader has a lot to do with attitude. It's about being confident, trustworthy, decisive, reliable, assertive, and consistent. A wild canine pack would never follow an aggressive or violent alpha dog because aggression is a sign of instability. Great Danes also do not respect bullies. To be a great canine leader, all you really need to do is think about the type of boss for whom you'd love to work, because that's the type of person your dog wants to work for too.

Your Great Dane appreciates firm but fair treatment. He views consistency as a form of security. He doesn't mind letting an assertive, decisive leader take control because then he doesn't have to worry about shouldering that responsibility

Your Great Dane will appreciate firm but fair treatment when it comes to training.

himself. And most importantly, he loves to receive rewards for doing a good job. Even dogs deserve a pat on the back once in a while! So treat your Great Dane firmly but kindly.

Communication

Food rewards are one of the greatest developments in dog training. Gone are the days when we had to physically force a dog into a *sit* or *down* to teach him what we wanted him to do; we can now use food to lure a dog into these positions. In addition, food helps keep dogs focused and motivated to learn. It allows us to train dogs faster and easier. Best of all, it makes training fun and enjoyable for both dog and trainer.

When we use food to reward a dog for correct behavior, we are communicating to the dog "Yes, that's what I want you to

Food rewards are often very effective when training the Great Dane.

do!" It only takes a few rewards for a dog to understand that, when he does things right, it's beneficial to him. From that point on, he'll put a lot of enthusiasm into attempting to earn more such rewards.

Sometimes, though, a breakdown occurs with this type of communication. The dog needs to be able to associate the reward with the desired behavior, or else he won't know what he's doing right. This means that he needs to receive the food reward while he is engaged in the desired behavior. But what happens if you can't get the reward to him at just the right moment? Maybe you can't get a treat out of your pocket fast enough, and by the time you do, your dog is no longer exhibiting the behavior you'd like to reward. Clicker training addresses this problem.

Clicker Training

Clicker training involves using a handheld noisemaker to produce a clicking sound whenever a dog is performing a desired behavior. A food reward always follows the sound of the click. This provides a bridge between the behavior and the delivery of a reward, as the dog quickly learns that the click, rather than the food, now means "Yes, that's what I want you to do!"

Marker Word

You don't necessarily need a clicker to use this superior method of communication with your dog. You can also use your voice. Issue the word "yes!" instead of a click, but always use the same upbeat tone of voice. After following this cue with a few food rewards, your dog will begin to think of it as the "magic word." It takes a little practice to get into the habit of using this word in training—you have to be consistent and exercise good timing—but you'll be amazed at how much quicker your dog learns what you want.

A couple of other voice cues that make it easier to communicate with your dog include a sharp displeasure cue, like "uh uh" or "shht," and an acknowledgment of good behavior, like "good" or "good boy." The purpose of the former is to tell your dog to stop what he's doing, and the purpose of the latter is to let your dog know when he is doing the right thing in cases when a food reward will not be forthcoming. Your consistent use of language can boost the level of communication you enjoy with your dog, but avoid talking to your dog as if he were a human—it only sounds like a lot of babbling to him, and your voice will eventually become meaningless white noise. Some of the best trainers in the world use verbal language very sparingly with their dogs.

Socialization

Not all the training you do with your dog will involve teaching him specific skills. He is constantly learning, even when you are not actively training him. Puppies, in particular, learn a lot about the world around them as they go through various developmental stages. You should be aware of these stages so that you can positively influence these early learning opportunities.

Puppies go through a very critical developmental stage between the ages of 6 and 12 weeks. They learn social, survival, and coping skills. But they can only learn these skills in relation to the environment in which they live. Puppies who do not receive exposure to other

Dogs should be socialized to people and to other dogs.

FINDING A TRAINER

Finding a good trainer is just as important as finding a good veterinarian. The best way to evaluate a trainer is in person. Reputable trainers always welcome potential clients to sit in and observe one of their classes. Make note of the following:

- Does the trainer use positive training techniques?
- Does the trainer work well with both people and dogs?
- Does the trainer communicate in ways that are easy to understand?
- How does the trainer handle training issues that arise? Does she offer alternative training techniques?
- Does the trainer appear to be knowledgeable about canine behavior?
- Does the trainer promote effective canine leadership?
- Is the trainer a member of a professional organization, such as the Association of Pet Dog Trainers (APDT), the National Association of Dog Obedience Instructors (NADOI), or the International Association of Animal Behavior Consultants (IAABC)?
- Do the class participants and their dogs appear comfortable and upbeat?
- Does the trainer appear to produce positive results?

dogs during this stage may not have the opportunity to develop good social skills with other dogs. If they never see a cat, they may not tolerate cats very well as adults. As part of their survival instincts, puppies in this age group also develop a natural fear of unfamiliar things. Even if raised by humans, a puppy may develop a fear of men in hats or children if they've never seen or interacted with these kinds of humans. If their exposure to unfamiliar things is painful or frightening, puppies may develop more serious, deep-rooted fears of those things.

New situations can also become a source of fear. Puppies who are isolated from the outside world do not have the opportunity to develop the coping skills necessary to handle new situations. These puppies may grow up to be dogs who are nervous at the dog park, too scared to go for walks, or have an extremely difficult time adjusting to a new home.

How to Socialize

To prevent your Great Dane puppy from developing these types of fears and to give your pup opportunities to develop important life skills, it's very important to give him a variety of experiences during this development period. Take your puppy out to meet lots of different people. Let him see lots of new places. And always make sure that these experiences are pleasant for your impressionable pup!

It's good for your Great Dane puppy to play with other friendly dogs too, but keep your dog's size in mind. If your Great Dane puppy is approaching his adult height, always supervise him around his smaller companions. Dogs tend to play roughly, and you'll have to make sure that your Great Dane's playmates can hold their own. Also, be aware that your dog's size may intimidate some dogs and lead to confrontations. Some smaller dogs, too, have no clue as to their size disparity with Great Danes and tend to instigate challenges. Always be prepared to protect your young Great Dane from such bad experiences.

Crate Training

A pet crate can provide a temporary confinement area for your puppy when you can't supervise him. It can provide a safe way to transport your dog in a vehicle or to separate your pets at feeding time. It can also be an invaluable aid in housetraining. But regardless of which of these reasons you choose to use a crate, it's not a very practical tool if your dog fusses incessantly whenever you confine him to it.

How to Crate Train

Teach your dog to accept the crate as his own special place by introducing him to it slowly. Dogs have a natural instinct to seek out cozy, den-like places to recline, so it's just a matter of convincing your dog that the crate is such a place. Put a dog bed or a crate pad in it to make it soft and enticing. Put a couple of your dog's favorite toys in it. Make the crate as comfortable as possible to encourage your dog to spend time in it.

Persuade your dog to investigate the crate by putting a few treats in front of it. Then try putting some treats just inside the crate door. As your dog becomes comfortable with putting his head inside the crate to get the treats, put some treats farther inside to convince him to enter it. When your dog seems perfectly at ease coming and going from his crate, start closing the crate door and confining your dog for short periods.

For the first few confinement sessions, give your dog some type of long-lasting chew item, like a dental chew or food-stuffed toy, to keep him busy. As soon as he's done chewing, release him from the crate. Increase your dog's confinement time gradually, and do not attempt to progress too fast. However, if your dog does start to whine, paw, or bark to get out, it's very important not to release him until he quiets down. Otherwise, you will be rewarding the behavior you are trying to train him not to do!

Your dog will eventually regard his crate as his own personal space, but regardless of how comfortable and secure he feels in it, it is not kind or healthy to confine your dog to a crate for more than six hours at a time. If you need to confine your dog for longer periods, it is best to keep him in a dog-safe room or ex-pen.

A good schedule and reasonable expectations will make housetraining your Great Dane easier.

Housetraining

Housetraining is not the odious endeavor it seems to be. All you really need are the right techniques and reasonable expectations. Great Danes are generally easy to housetrain, but you should remember that very young dogs have limited bladder control. You cannot expect them to succeed at housetraining until they are mentally and physically mature enough to do it, which may be anywhere from three to six months of age in most cases. In situations where a dog has already developed bad house manners, it may take even longer. But regardless of your dog's history, the same basic concepts apply to housetraining any dog: prevention, planning, and incentives.

How to Housetrain

Prevention can help you prevent household accidents. This alone can significantly reduce the stress factor in housetraining! You must supervise your dog closely when he is about the house and keep him in a confined area, such as a crate, ex-pen, or safe room, when you cannot supervise him. It's hard for your dog to develop the bad habit of soiling your house if he never has the opportunity to do it.

Always make sure that your dog has a potty break prior to confinement. Puppies may require an appropriate indoor area to do their duty, especially if you need to confine a puppy for more than an hour or two. Newspapers or puppy pads can designate an appropriate spot within your puppy's confinement area, and you can eventually stop using them when your puppy has matured sufficiently and learned to potty outside. Because the scent of a previously soiled area stimulates a puppy to do his business, manufacturers treat puppy pads with a similar scent that encourages puppies to use them. You can achieve this same effect with newspapers by saving a piece of soiled newspaper to lay down with the clean supply each time you clean up after your dog.

Your dog's instinct to reuse a previously soiled area is a double-edged sword. On the one hand, if your dog has an accident in the house, that spot will be a magnet for more accidents. This is why you must clean up any household accidents with a product specifically designed to neutralize pet odors. But on the other hand, you can use this canine instinct to your advantage in establishing an appropriate outdoor potty area.

This is where planning comes in. You must choose a specific outdoor area to take your dog for potty breaks, and plan to take your dog there when he is most likely to need it. Dogs often need to eliminate after eating, napping, or playing. Hopefully, you'll have your dog on a regular schedule with these activities, so he'll be on a regular potty schedule as well. To make it easy for your dog to learn to "hold it," he has to know when to expect the next break.

Sometimes the key to successfully housetraining a dog requires an incentive to get your message across. Dogs find it much easier to go whenever and wherever the urge hits them. What reason does your dog have to hold it until he gets outside? Food rewards can help provide the incentive he needs. If you reward your dog for his successes, he'll put a lot more effort into doing things your way.

No matter how diligent you are, a few accidents are sure to happen. If you catch your dog attempting to go in the house, rush him outside to his potty spot. It's not fair to punish your dog for something he hasn't

Choose a specific outdoor area to take your dog for potty breaks.

To keep your dog safe, practice the *come* command constantly, beyond your regular training sessions.

mastered yet; worse, such unjust treatment can undermine your dog's trust in you. So be kind to your dog during housetraining. With prevention, planning, and wonderful incentives, you'll have a housetrained Great Dane before you know it!

Basic Obedience Commands

It's obvious that when you bring such a colossal canine into your life, you have to train him. But how do you convince an animal that outruns, overpowers, and possibly outweighs you to do what you want him to do? Humans have succeeded in training animals much larger than your Great Dane, thanks to a superior intellect.

It's good to keep this in mind when training your dog, as training is really a mental exercise, not a physical one.

Basic obedience training consists of teaching your dog the minimum skills required for you to gain control of his behavior. Basic obedience is also a stepping stone for many other activities and training endeavors. But just like any other type of education, your dog will forget his training if he doesn't practice his skills once in a while.

In the beginning, try to schedule at least three training sessions per week. You can train even more frequently if you wish, as long as the sessions are not too close together and your dog doesn't start getting too porky on training treats. (Always remember to adjust your dog's diet to compensate for the food he consumes during training.)

The length of your training sessions should be appropriate for the age of your dog. Puppies have short attention spans and usually can't tolerate more than ten minutes of training at a time. Adult dogs can stay focused for up to 20 minutes. These training sessions should be fun activities that both you and your dog look forward to.

After your dog has learned a basic obedience skill and appears to be performing it consistently, it's important to phase out the food rewards. Basic obedience is not a "tricks for treats" proposition. When your dog learns the *sit* command, for example, begin rewarding him every other time he performs a *sit*. Then, after a while, cut back to rewarding him every three or four times he obeys this command. Eventually, you can wean your dog off treats altogether.

Once your dog has mastered basic obedience commands, invest in his continuing education. Make a habit of reviewing his lessons once every week or two, and think of something new to teach him occasionally. This will help keep his skills in top form, keep his mind active, and condition him to be responsive to you. Great Danes are generally willing and attentive pupils. But keep in mind that if you have a young, squirmy Great Dane who has too much energy to concentrate on what you are trying to teach him, you'll need to take him for a walk or exercise

him before training sessions. This will help to settle your dog down so that you can gain his undivided attention.

Come

A dog who does not come when called is an accident waiting to happen. He could become lost, hit by a car, poisoned, or worse. Complicating your efforts to train your dog is the fact that young dogs can be somewhat rebellious, and they have a tremendous urge to explore. Due to the potentially serious consequences for a dog who does not recall reliably, you should practice the *come* command constantly, beyond your regular training sessions.

How to Teach *Come*

First, practice in the house. Carry treats with you or have them available at different locations around your home. Call

Ask the Expert

SPECIAL TRAINING CONSIDERATIONS

Q: Are there any special considerations in training an extra-large dog like the Great Dane?

A: "Large breeds can go through some awkward growth stages. It's important to notice when it becomes cumbersome for the dog to sit, for example, and to work around these stages when training, sometimes waiting until the dog's body is more agile and less awkward. Also, trainers should not be fooled by the size of the dog. Giant breeds are mentally and physically immature for several years, despite their large size."

—Carol Lea Benjamin, author of *Mother Knows Best: The Natural Way to Train Your Dog* your dog frequently from different rooms, and reward him when he responds. Only call your dog once each time. If he doesn't come on one call, he shouldn't get any rewards. This way, your dog will learn to pay attention and respond the first time you call him.

After your dog responds to the *come* command consistently indoors, it's time to train him outdoors where there are a lot more distractions. Work with your dog in a fenced area or attach a long line to his collar to keep him safe. When working with a long line, do not use the line to force your dog to come if he does not respond to the command. This is the fastest way to teach your dog that compliance is only mandatory if he is on a leash.

Wait until your dog is distracted, then call him to you. Again, call only once. If he comes, he gets a reward; if he doesn't come, he misses out on a fabulous treat. You can encourage your dog to come by running away from him and calling him to you in a happy, excited voice. With lots and lots of practice, you can condition your dog to respond to this command automatically.

Make sure that your dog recalls reliably while in an enclosed area or on a long line before attempting to train him in the open. The first few times, you can have another person assist you by holding your dog's leash and releasing your dog

to come to you as he responds to your command. You can also allow your dog to explore a short distance away from you with his long line dragging on the ground. Then, if he doesn't respond to your *come* command, it will be easier to catch him and prevent him from running off.

Sit

The *sit* position is very useful for grooming your dog or trimming his nails. Also, a dog can't jump on people, run away, or engage in other undesirable behaviors from a *sit* position.

How to Teach *Sit*

You can teach your dog this valuable skill by holding a treat a few inches (cm) above your dog's head. While your dog is looking up at the treat, move the treat slowly toward his back. If your dog sits in order to keep his eyes on the treat, issue a "Yes!" and let him have the reward. You can then start using the *sit* command so that your dog can associate it with the *sit* position.

If your dog keeps jumping up to get the treat instead of sitting during this exercise, you may be holding the treat too high. Hold the treat closer to your dog's head. Most dogs learn this command quite quickly.

Down

The next logical step is to teach your dog the *down*, as this command is easiest

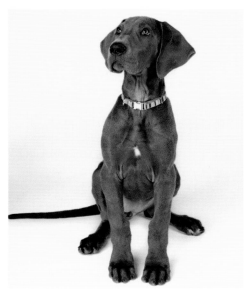

The *sit* position is useful and easy for most dogs to learn.

to teach with your dog starting in a *sit* position.

How to Teach *Down*

Crouch in front of your sitting dog and hold a treat on the floor in front of him. While your dog is sniffing at your hand, slowly pull the treat along the floor away from him. If your dog moves either front foot toward you without breaking his sitting position, issue a "Yes!" and let him have the reward. If he breaks his *sit* position, you'll have to make him sit again and start over.

Some skills, like the *down*, are easier for your dog to master if you teach them in small increments. At first, reward any tiny bit of progress in the right direction. You can then ask your dog to stretch out more and more in pursuit of the treat until he eventually drops into a full *down*. When your dog has achieved a full *down*, start using the verbal *down* command.

Stay

The *stay* is another skill that requires a gradual introduction.

How to Teach *Stay*

With your dog in a *sit* position, instruct him to stay and take a quick step away from him. The hand signal for *stay* (a raised hand with the palm facing the dog) may help encourage your dog to hold still. Step back toward your dog immediately and reward him if has maintained his position.

Gradually increase the distance and duration of your dog's *stay*, and reward him for his successes. If your dog breaks a *stay*, you may be progressing too fast, in which case you'll need to shorten the distance and duration of the *stay* so that your dog can master this skill at an easier level before your progress to something harder. It is important to walk back to your dog to reward him. If you call your dog to come to you for his reward, he'll learn that *stay* means "stay for a little while and then come," and he'll never

Gradually increase the distance and duration of your dog's *stay*, and reward him for his successes.

learn to maintain a *stay* for very long. Wait until your dog has mastered a good solid *stay* before you start releasing him by calling him to you. You can also issue an "Okay" to let your dog know that the exercise is over.

Eventually, progress to out-of-sight *stays*. Approach this training with very short durations in the beginning. Take one step out of the room and return immediately to reward your dog for staying put. Pretty soon, you'll be able to walk across the entire house with your dog remaining firmly planted!

Leash Manners

Taking your Great Dane for walks is great for your dog's mental and physical health. You'll find that it's fun to be out and about with a Great Dane, as they often become neighborhood celebrities. But it's not such a wonderful activity if your Great Dane uses his brute strength to pull your shoulder out of its socket. Leash training is an absolute must for such a large, powerful canine.

Most problems with leash training revolve around consistency, because people often attempt to take their dogs for walks before they are leash trained. It's hard to be consistent in not allowing a dog to pull if there is a specific distance to cover and a specific time to cover it. If you want a well-mannered dog at the end of your leash, train your dog first. Every time your dog is on a leash, it should be considered a training session. Once your dog understands what you expect, you can reinforce what he has learned by taking him for regular walks.

How to Teach Leash Manners

Take your dog out in the yard on his leash, and if he pulls, make an abrupt turn and walk in the opposite direction. When your dog catches up to your side, praise him and reward him for the slack leash. If you want to teach your dog the more precise position of *heel*, encourage him to stay at your left side by holding a treat

Check It Out

TRAINING CHECKLIST

✓ Use only positive training methods with your Great Dane.

✓ Use fairness, firmness, and consistency to become an effective canine leader.

✓ Use your voice or a clicker to communicate effectively with your dog.

✓ Socialize your dog to as many different types of people and animals as possible.

✓ Make your dog's first social encounters positive experiences.

✓ Introduce your dog to a crate slowly and positively.

✓ Confine your puppy to a safe area when you can't supervise him.

✓ Supervise your puppy closely when he is not confined.

✓ Establish an outdoor potty area.

✓ Keep your puppy on a regular potty break schedule.

✓ Limit training sessions to 10 minutes for puppies and 20 minutes for adult dogs.

✓ Plan at least three obedience training sessions per week until your dog is trained.

✓ Give your dog continuing education to keep his skills intact.

✓ Seek professional advice, if necessary, to get your dog's behavior under control.

in your left hand and rewarding your dog occasionally for maintaining his position there. It won't take long for him to figure out that it is much more profitable for him to stay close to you rather than pulling.

If you have a persistent puller, it's very important to get your Great Dane's behavior under control. Do not hesitate to consult with a professional trainer to find a training method or training appliance that will help you achieve positive results. Obedience training classes can be a worthwhile investment in your Great Dane's future. Having the opportunity to train amid the distraction of other dogs is invaluable, and the guidance of a professional trainer can make the training process easier for both you and your dog.

Regular training sessions are a great way to "keep in tune" with your canine friend. Training improves communication and contributes to a greater understanding between you and your dog. Most importantly, it allows you to establish the kind of relationship dogs and humans were meant to have—a partnership.

Chapter
7

Solving Problems with
Your Great Dane

Living with a Great Dane is like living with an alien. If you've ever watched the old sitcoms *Mork & Mindy* or *My Favorite Martian*, you know that living with an alien species involves challenges. Dogs don't look like we do. They don't think like we do. They don't act like we do.

For the most part, we manage to get along with them, but there are times when those differences can cause problems. Some people choose to tolerate problem behaviors simply because they do not think that there is a reasonable solution to them. The truth is that almost all canine problem behaviors are solvable. Life with a Great Dane should be fun and enjoyable, not frustrating and stressful!

Life with a Great Dane should be fun and enjoyable, not frustrating and stressful.

Problem Solving

Every dog is different and every situation is different, which means that there isn't always a single perfect solution that applies to all situations. It may take some creativity on your part to come up with a reasonable solution that you and your dog can live with. The following topics will give you some angles from which to approach various problem behaviors.

Meet Your Dog's Needs

Think of your dog's behavior as his way of communicating his needs to you. What is he trying to say by behaving that way? If your dog jumps on you when you come home from work, he may be saying "I'm excited to see you, and I need to express my happiness." If this is the case, you can solve the problem by finding a more acceptable way for your dog to release his excitement upon your return home.

You may have to put your dog's behavior in context to determine exactly what he's trying to say. If your dog chews on the furniture, he may be saying "I'm bored, and I need something to do." But he may also be trying to indicate that he's teething, and he needs to chew on something to relieve the discomfort. Determining what your dog needs can help you find appropriate ways to meet those needs and eliminate problem behaviors.

PARENTING A PUPPY

Many parenting techniques that are effective with children are also effective with puppies. Use the following techniques to help influence your puppy's behavior:

Time-out: A time-out can consist of simply ignoring your puppy for a few minutes or placing him in his puppy pen or crate for a few minutes. This is very effective in helping a puppy calm down if his overexcitement causes him to play inappropriately or makes him lose self-control in other ways.

Redirection: When your puppy engages in inappropriate behavior, always redirect him to a more appropriate behavior. This will help teach him what to do in place of the inappropriate behavior.

Ignoring whining: Behaviors that are annoying will cease when they no longer generate the attention your puppy is seeking.

Positive reinforcement: You may already give your dog plenty of positive reinforcement in the form of treats during training, but what about all the times when you don't have treats? Make a conscious effort to "catch your dog being good" and praise him for it. This includes times when he plays nicely with another household pet, walks nicely on the leash, or waits patiently for his dinner. This will go a long way toward nurturing your dog's will to please and creating a well-mannered pet.

Provide Enough Exercise

One of the needs most often expressed by dogs through inappropriate behavior is a need for more exercise. Dogs who don't get enough exercise tend to develop all sorts of problem behaviors. Some people think that Great Danes are supposed to lounge around like giant stuffed teddy bears all day, and they are surprised to discover that their young Great Dane has some very robust bursts of energy.

Provide some form of physical exercise on a daily basis. Dogs who can count on getting a good aerobic workout once a day tend to conserve their energy (and therefore stay out of trouble) during other times of the day. If your dog's undesirable behavior is a result of excess energy, a regular exercise session can help subdue the "wild thing" in him. Dogs are crepuscular, which means that they are most active during the morning and evening hours. Plan your exercise sessions during these times to get the most benefit from them.

Make Appropriate Concessions

You can't blame a dog for being a dog. Dogs are scavengers. It's natural for them to get into the garbage, so keep your garbage receptacle in an inaccessible place. If you put food on an end table and leave the room, you can bet that your Great Dane will help himself in your absence. It is not fair to punish a dog for being a dog. Although he may show a measure of self-control in your presence, you cannot expect him to exhibit the same self-control when you are out of the picture.

Also, you can't blame a Great Dane for being humongous. Remember, he is large enough to prewash the dirty dishes in your sink. He's tall enough to reach anything on the kitchen counters, and he can probably reach things even higher than that. Your Great Dane also can't help the fact that his tail can wipe out a whole row of flowerpots in a single wag of happiness. Being diligent about keeping things out of your big dog's reach and rearranging your furnishings when necessary can help prevent problems. Try to recognize when your dog can't help causing a problem, and see if there is a concession you can make to prevent its recurrence.

Use Pet-Parenting Skills

Just like parenting a child, raising a well-behaved, well-adjusted dog requires good pet-parenting skills. Although children and pets are both very good at coming up with new challenging behaviors to keep us on our toes, whether or not those behaviors persist to become habits depends entirely on how we deal with them.

Setting clear-cut boundaries and being consistent in enforcing them is very important. What many people don't realize, though, is that consistency must apply in every situation. For instance, if you are consistent in not allowing your dog to jump on you when you get home from work but you allow your dog to jump on you while playing, you may be sabotaging your own training efforts. Teach your Great Dane to respect your personal space in all situations.

If you've tried to solve a problem behavior but your dog just doesn't seem to be getting the message, try to figure out why. Is there something you are doing (or not doing) that is contributing to the problem? Have you been a good canine leader, so that your dog respects you? Have you used proven training techniques? Have you been as consistent as possible? Have you tried supervision and confinement to prevent problems?

Keep a Sense of Humor

Don't let your emotions get in the way of solving a problem. It's easy to become so flustered that you can't see a solution even when it's right in front of you. It's also easy to overreact and discipline your dog unfairly. Just remember that someday you're going to laugh about your dog's misdeeds, and when your faithful friend passes on, you might even recall them with fondness.

Always keep things in perspective and recognize that dogs do not misbehave in order to distress us. They are simply acting like the alien species they are—canines. Take a good dose of patience and a couple shots of perseverance. And if that doesn't help, make an appointment with a professional trainer or animal behaviorist.

Common Problem Behaviors

Finding a solution for a problem is often a matter of searching hard enough. The following suggestions can get you started in solving some common problem behaviors.

Aggression

Aggression is quite different from play biting, which is discussed later. A dog who bites out of aggression does so with the purposeful attempt to harm. A Great Dane who bites can do a serious amount of damage to a human or animal. Because of this, any form of aggression, no matter how "minor," requires major attention.

Don't let your emotions get in the way of solving a problem with your Great Dane.

There are several different forms of aggression. Some dogs are aggressive toward people. Some dogs seem perfectly fine with humans, but they are aggressive toward other dogs. Some dogs are only aggressive when protecting their food. Some dogs are aggressive out of dominance, while other dogs are aggressive out of fear and insecurity.

How to Manage It

For your own safety and the safety of others, always consult a professional trainer or animal behaviorist to help you deal with aggression. This is a

PROFESSIONAL TRAINING ASSISTANCE

Q: When should a pet owner seek professional training assistance?

A: "Pet owners should seek professional help when they can't get the dog trained on their own, or if they see any signs of aggression that they have any doubts about handling on their own."

—Carol Lea Benjamin, author of *Mother Knows Best: The Natural Way to Train Your Dog*

complicated problem that may require an analysis of your household dynamics to solve. If possible, choose a professional who specializes in canine aggression, and always ask for references. Choosing someone without the right credentials could possibly make things worse.

There are some things you can do, however, to help prevent your dog from developing aggressive tendencies. First, be an effective canine leader. Dogs who have trustworthy and respect-worthy owners have less reason to be dominant or fearful. Second, socialize your Great Dane as much as possible. Many dogs become dog-aggressive simply because they've lived in a human "pack" their entire lives, and they've never had the opportunity to develop good social skills with other dogs.

Dogs who are not accustomed to children may be made uneasy by a child's boisterous, reckless, or noisy play. If you do not have children of your own, it is a good idea to invite well-behaved children to come over and play with your Great Dane puppy (under supervision, of course). It will have a lifelong influence on how your dog perceives and reacts to children.

Begging

Begging can be a huge problem with Great Danes, and there is absolutely no pun intended here. If your Great Dane begs, he will be literally drooling in your mashed potatoes. He'll be at an intimidating eye level to your seated guests. It's no fun to have a monster canine moocher at your table.

How to Manage It

The easiest way to get your dog to stop begging is to teach him the *place* command. Find a place within sight of the table where your dog can lie down without being an obstruction. Outside of mealtimes, lead your dog to that spot frequently and practice a *down-stay*. Instruct your dog to lie down at the designated spot and issue a *stay* command. Reward your dog if he maintains his *down* position for just a few seconds. Each time you take him to that spot and practice a *down-stay*, require your dog to maintain his position there for a longer period before you reward him. You can eventually start pointing to that spot and using the *place* command. When your dog seems to have the hang of this, try it at mealtimes.

Be prepared to interrupt your meal to enforce this new rule. Your dog will adjust to it more easily if you reward him occasionally for maintaining his *down-stay*. With firm, consistent training, you will soon enjoy slobber-free meals. Your dog may even begin to take his "place" automatically at mealtimes.

Barking (Excessive)

Great Danes are not yappy dogs. Some of them aren't even very good watchdogs because they are not always on high alert to every little sound. Still, it pays to teach your Great Dane that his barking serves a very important purpose and that it's not acceptable to "cry wolf" or carry on incessantly every time the mail carrier comes by.

How to Manage It

Whenever your dog barks an alert, make an effort to check out what his commotion

Begging can be a problem with a Great Dane, especially because he'll be at eye level to your seated guests.

is all about. Whether he sees people or animals or strange motorized vehicles, praise your dog for alerting you to the "problem" and then tell him that everything is okay. This is an indication for your dog to stop barking. If you have earned your dog's respect, he will trust your judgment that there is nothing to worry about.

Be reasonable in your expectations. If a strange man is approaching your door, you can't very well expect your Great Dane to stop barking while a "threatening" stimulus is still approaching. But if your dog is barking at some children playing across the street, and you've made it clear to him that everything is okay, the barking should stop.

If the barking doesn't stop, issue a firm *quiet* command. Give your dog a reward if he remains quiet for at least five seconds. As your dog figures out what this command means, require longer periods of silence before giving your dog a reward.

If your Great Dane gets in the habit of barking at "nothing," respond to his alert and then act very disappointed in his poor performance as a guardian. Do not give him praise or rewards for false alerts. Soon your dog will realize what an important job he has, and he'll take it much more seriously.

Always keep in mind that barking is a form of communication. If you pay attention to your dog's barks, you will become familiar with which barks mean "I think I heard something" and which ones mean "There is definitely a problem here." If your dog barks constantly in your absence, he may be indicating that he is bored or lonely, in which case you'll have to take steps to improve his living situation. Enrollment in a doggy day care facility or midday visits from a professional pet sitter may help.

Chewing

Chewing generally has nothing to do with your Great Dane's appetite. There are already plenty of other reasons for dogs to chew. Puppies need to chew to relieve the discomforts of teething. Adult dogs chew to clean their teeth. Sometimes dogs chew to relieve stress or boredom. You can address most of these situations with adequate prevention and training.

How to Manage It

Make sure that your dog has plenty of appropriate things of his own to chew, such as a Nylabone. Items that offer a variety of sizes, shapes, textures, and hardness will give him ample choices to please his particular tastes and satisfy his various moods. Keep these items in a central location, like a toy box, so that your dog knows where to find them.

Until your puppy learns which items are appropriate to chew on and which items are not, do not leave anything on the floor that you do not want him to chew. This means putting away shoes, children's toys, and anything else that typically litters the floor. Of course, you can't remove your furnishings, so you'll have to supervise your puppy carefully at first to see if he targets those things with his teeth.

If you catch your puppy chewing on something inappropriate, issue a firm "No!" and then distract him with one of his own chew toys. If there is a particular piece of furniture that your chomping pup really can't seem to resist, try a deterrent. Bitter-tasting sprays or indoor boundary sprays are available at most pet supply stores.

Dogs who chew due to stress when left alone may suffer from separation anxiety.

Great Danes, being fairly laid-back fellows, aren't as prone to this problem as more excitable breeds, but dogs of any breed often experience some anxiety when adjusting to a new home. If your dog tends to chew things up in your absence, confine him to a safe area before you leave the house and give him a long-lasting chew product to placate him. Food-stuffed toys work great for this purpose.

Digging

Unlike some dog breeds, Great Danes do not have a burning desire to dig. The only

WHERE TO SEEK PROFESSIONAL HELP

Most canine behavioral issues can be resolved. The following resources are available for Great Dane owners in distress:

- Contact local animal shelters to see if they have an animal behaviorist on staff who can provide free advice.
- Contact Great Dane rescue groups because they are familiar with the breed and are a good source of information. Many of these groups are listed on www. petfinder.com or the Great Dane Club of America (GDCA) website at www. gdca.org.
- Contact a local Great Dane breed club to see if its members may be of assistance. Great Dane clubs are listed on the GDCA website at www.gdca.org.
- Consult a professional trainer. Check the website of the Association of Pet Dog Trainers (APDT) at www.apdt.com or the National Association of Dog Obedience Instructors (NADOI) at www.nadoi.org for referrals.
- Consult a professional animal behaviorist. Visit the website for the International Association of Animal Behavior Consultants (IAABC) at www.iaabc.org to see its membership list.
- Check with your veterinarian. Your veterinarian can rule out health-related causes for problem behaviors or provide a referral to a veterinary behaviorist (a veterinarian who specializes in animal behavior).
- Consult a veterinary behaviorist. You can find veterinarians who specialize in this field by visiting the website of the American College of Veterinary Behaviorists (ACVB) at www.veterinarybehaviorists.org or the American Veterinary Society of Animal Behavior (AVSAB) at www.avsabonline.org.

time a Great Dane enjoys digging is when there is nothing better to do, when he's trying to find a cool place to lie down, or when he's trying to extract vermin from a hole.

How to Manage It

The first two scenarios are relatively easy to remedy: Don't leave your Great Dane unattended outside for long periods. This is a recipe for boredom.

When your dog is outside, supervise him, and make sure that he has appropriate activities to keep him busy. Keep some durable toys outdoors for your dog to play with. He won't be digging up the flower garden for a cool spot to lie down if he can come indoors when he's done playing—your Great Dane much prefers his soft, comfy dog bed.

As for the rodents, your Great Dane would really like to help you get rid of them. But if you don't want your yard to look like a minefield, it might be best to pursue other methods of extermination. Consult a pest control expert to eliminate the source of the problem.

Jumping Up

Jumping up is a complicated problem compounded by the sheer size of a Great Dane. This behavior most often occurs when a dog attempts to greet humans, but it might also occur when your dog wants food, attention, or a toy in your hand. It is an excitement-driven behavior, which makes it very self-rewarding for the dog. When a dog jumps, he is able to release some of that excitement, and that feels good to him.

How to Manage It

Teaching your dog not to jump up involves enforcing your personal space. Alpha canines do not tolerate blatant invasions of their personal space, and you shouldn't either. You want to begin teaching your Great Dane puppy to respect your body before he grows into a giant deadly projectile.

The techniques used to discourage your dog from jumping up depend on the situation. When greeting your dog after an absence, keep things calm and quiet so that you do not heighten his excitement. Turn your back on him and issue a displeasure cue, like "Uh uh," if he attempts to jump on you. Refuse to give your dog any attention for this behavior.

You can also instruct your dog to sit before greeting him, but for some dogs, it's not reasonable to expect them to sit calmly when they are in an excited state of mind. If your dog needs to expend some of his exuberance before he can settle down, encourage him to fetch one of his toys. Throw his ball a few times so that he can release some of his energy reserves. If you get in the habit of doing this whenever you walk in the door, your dog may begin to greet you with a toy instead of jumping on you. It's all about meeting your dog's need to release his excitement in an appropriate way.

If your dog jumps on you while playing, stop playing for a few seconds. If you are playing fetch and your dog jumps on you to get the ball or flying disc in your hand, turn away from him, issue your displeasure cue, and wait until your dog's paws are on the floor for a few seconds before throwing the toy again. He will quickly learn that the game stops when he doesn't respect your personal space.

Enforce your personal space in other situations as well. Do not allow your Great Dane to climb all over you. Although it may appear to be your dog's innocent expression of affection, it is a very disrespectful way for your dog to show his affection. Your dog should not touch your body unless you invite him to do so. Dogs who do not respect personal space can become pushy and dominant. Great Danes who do not respect personal space can be just plain hazardous! Go ahead and enjoy close physical contact with your large furry friend, but be sure to do it on your own terms.

Play Biting

Dogs and puppies bite each other in play all the time. That doesn't mean that it's okay for them to play with humans that way. Play biting can quickly become painful and cause injury when a dog becomes overly aroused in play. It is best

Dogs who chew due to stress when left alone may suffer from separation anxiety.

not to allow or encourage your dog to put his teeth on you.

How to Manage It

If your dog tries to bite you in play, offer him an appropriate biting toy, like a tug rope, instead. If he still tries to bite your hands, feet, or body, the most effective consequence is to stop playing with him for a moment. This doggy "time-out" will give your Great Dane a chance to calm down and get his behavior under control. It will also teach him that the fun stops when he bites.

Running Away

Running away can be a frustrating problem simply because dogs run faster than humans. If your dog doesn't want you to catch him, you won't catch him. Fortunately, Great Danes tend to be devout homebodies. But if you have recently acquired your Great Dane or your dog is going through the exploratory period between six months and two years of age, you might find yourself in the position of chasing down your fugitive canine.

How to Manage It

Prevention can help you avoid such a predicament. Practice the *come* command constantly, and keep your dog on a leash or in a fenced area when outdoors until he learns to recall reliably. But no matter what precautions you take, there is always a chance that your dog may get loose. What will you do if your dog gets out the door when people are coming and going? What will you do if he jumps out of the car before you manage to get a leash on him?

You can prevent these scenarios by teaching your dog the *wait* command. With your dog on a leash, stand by the door and instruct him to wait. Open the door just a crack and be prepared to shut the door quickly or block the door with your body to prevent your dog from rushing out. If your dog gets past you, you'll have to pull him back with the leash and start over. If he doesn't rush the door, shut the door and reward him. Begin opening the door wider and wider, and reward your dog when he waits properly.

When you can get the door open wide enough to pass through it, release your dog with an "Okay" so that he can go through the door. Practice making your dog wait and then giving him the okay to pass through the door. Next, practice this skill at other doors in your home. Practice it at the vet's office, or when getting in and out of the car. Having a dog with door manners can make your life much easier!

It takes time to train a dog. So what do you do if your dog gets loose before he's had enough training? There are a few tricks you can use to get your dog back. Try running away from your dog and calling him in an excited voice. Dogs love

Dogs and puppies bite each other in play all the time, but that doesn't mean that it's okay for them to play with humans that way.

Check It Out

PROBLEM BEHAVIORS CHECKLIST

✓ Solve problem behaviors by meeting your dog's needs, making concessions when necessary, being persistent, and keeping a sense of humor.

✓ Be very consistent in not sharing your food with your Great Dane.

✓ Make sure that your dog has plenty of his own chew toys so that he doesn't chew on inappropriate items.

✓ Don't leave your dog unsupervised outside for long periods.

✓ Give your dog plenty of toys and activities to keep him busy both indoors and outdoors.

✓ Teach your Great Dane to respect the personal space of humans.

✓ Take precautions to prevent your dog from running off until you have trained him to recall reliably.

✓ Give your dog a "time-out" if he plays too roughly.

✓ Seek professional help for behavior issues if necessary.

to play chase, and your dog may come running after you.

You can also entice your dog to come back by using words that get his attention, like "treat" or "walk." If your dog loves car rides, open your car door and invite him to go for a ride. When offering something your dog wants, be prepared to deliver on such promises. You should never, ever punish your dog when he comes to you, no matter how frustrated you are, because it will make him fearful to come to you the next time.

There may be times when it seems that even a T-bone steak won't entice your dog to come. Running is such a highly rewarding behavior that little else can compare. In this case, you may need to allow your dog to roam and explore for a little while before he'll be willing to come to you. Walk parallel to your dog so that

you don't encourage him to run farther away. When he's had a chance to get some of the roaming out of his system, try to coax him into following you home.

You can meet your dog's need to explore by taking your dog on regular walks. Dogs are pack animals, and your dog may just realize that it's more fun to "roam" with you than to do it alone!

Dogs may seem to be from another planet, but they are very receptive to down-to-earth training methods. It takes some effort to teach a dog how to behave in a human world, but this investment of time and energy is well worth the lifelong benefits they provide. Your Great Dane really wants to be the dog of your dreams because, when you're happy, he's happy!

Chapter
8

Activities With Your Great Dane

Great Danes are aesthetically beautiful, incredibly huge, and impressively strong, but these are not the greatest things your Great Dane has to offer. Much deeper and far more enduring are the companionship and lifelong memories your devoted Great Dane will provide.

Your dog would spend all of his time with you if he had the chance. He delights in walking with you, playing with you, lying next to you, traveling with you, and participating in just about anything you like to do. But your dog can only give you as much companionship as you allow him. He needs opportunities to make memories with you. If you want to get the most "greatness" out of your Great Dane experience, think of all of the different activities you and your dog can enjoy together!

Sports and Activities

Your Great Dane would love to share your passions with you. But on the other hand, you can just as easily enjoy the passions of your Great Dane. Does your dog show a talent or an interest in certain types of activities? Helping your dog reach his true potential, both physically and mentally, is one of the greatest ways to enjoy your dog.

Agility is a timed event in which dogs must navigate an obstacle course.

Agility

Agility is a fast-paced, exciting sport that is physically demanding for both dog and handler. The dog must overcome numerous obstacles on a course, including jumps, weave poles, tunnels, and climbing apparatus. And just to make the sport even more challenging, the dog must lie down on a "pause" table situated somewhere along the course. This takes an incredible amount of control because at this point the dog is usually overwhelmed with adrenaline.

This is a timed event in which the dogs who complete the course the fastest without any penalties are awarded. Because each agility course is different, you have to direct your dog to each obstacle in the correct order, and this will require a little bit of energy on your part. It can be exhausting attempting to keep up with a highly motivated dog on an agility course, so this is not a sport for couch potatoes.

It is also a time-consuming activity. You'll have to enroll in an agility training course, as it takes quite a bit of training to teach a dog how to traverse each obstacle efficiently and follow the direction of his handler. But training for this sport is just as rewarding as the competition itself. For many competitors, attending agility training classes is a social outlet, a canine bonding activity, and a physical workout all rolled into one.

Don't think that your Great Dane is too placid for such an aerobic sport. Great Danes are amazingly fast, energetic, and athletic, thanks to their sighthound ancestors. Some Great Danes are addicted to speed, and agility is the perfect outlet for them.

In addition to earning ribbons for first though fourth place, you can also earn agility titles for your dog. Different organizations issue different titles for this sport. The American Kennel Club (AKC), the North American Dog Agility Council (NADAC), the United States Dog Agility Association (USDAA), the United Kennel Club (UKC), and Canine Performance Events (CPE) sanction agility events in the United States. In Britain, the Kennel Club (KC) organizes all agility competitions.

Canine Musical Freestyle

Canine musical freestyle is a unique sport that has been evolving for more than a decade. Two types of canine musical freestyle have emerged over the years. Heelwork to Music is a more formal version of the sport that focuses on executing specific obedience-type maneuvers to music. Some people compare it to equestrian dressage. Canine Musical Freestyle is much less formal and often includes unique tricks and colorful costumes. This version of the sport is quite popular with spectators, as the

Ask the Expert

TRAVEL AGENTS

Q: Do some travel agents specialize in pet travel, and if so, how can pet owners locate them?

A: "Travel agents who specialize in the transport of pets worldwide are referred to as pet transporters or pet shippers. Certified pet transporters can be found on the Independent Pet and Animal Transportation Association (IPATA)'s website at www.ipata.com. IPATA pet shippers adhere to the rules and regulations of the International Air Transport Association (IATA), a global trade organization that represents more than 230 airlines worldwide."

—Susan H. Smith, President, Pet Travel, Inc.

participants have a lot of creative freedom in choreographing entertaining routines. Some routines are performed like dances (hence, the sport is often called "doggy dancing"), and some routines are more dramatic and tell a "story."

If you enjoy teaching your dog tricks as much as you enjoy showing him off, canine musical freestyle may be the sport for you. Great Danes attract a lot of attention in this sport simply because, well, you can imagine a giant dancing dog is quite a novelty. So if you enjoy being in the spotlight, check the World Canine Freestyle Organization's (WCFO) website at www.wcfo-dog.com for listings of Canine Musical Freestyle clubs near you. You can also check with local training facilities to see if they offer training classes in this sport. If it is difficult to find training opportunities in your area, books

and videos are always available through the WCFO's website.

Conformation (Dog Shows) and Breeding

Conformation dog shows offer the most prestigious honors for purebred dogs. This is where the best of the best are chosen as superior representatives of a breed. Dogs are compared against their respective breed standards as they compete against other dogs of the same breed. The dogs who exhibit the most exceptional physical and temperamental traits for their breed are then compared with top dogs in all the other breeds to compete for the highly coveted Best in Show award.

You might think that your Great Dane is the most beautiful canine creation in the world, but that doesn't mean that he can succeed in the show ring. It requires

In a dog show, the dog is evaluated against the breed standard.

a lot of planning and forethought to get involved in conformation showing. You need to decide if this sport interests you before you even acquire your dog because you need to choose a good-quality show dog prospect who has what it takes to compete against all of the other fabulous Great Danes.

In addition to the cost of a fine-quality dog, many other significant expenses are involved in this sport. There are travel expenses and entry fees. If you are not confident enough to show your own dog, you may have to pay a professional handler to show your dog for you. But the costs of competition are not the only considerations.

You'll also have to consider whether or not you are willing to live with an intact dog because show dogs cannot be neutered or spayed according to show regulations. It doesn't make much sense for a dog to achieve a championship if he cannot pass on his superb traits to the next generation of dogs. For this reason, showing and breeding tend to go together like peaches and cream.

Are you willing to take precautions to prevent your intact dog from producing unwanted litters of puppies? Are you prepared to deal with sexually motivated behaviors, such as urine marking (urinating on furniture) and roaming? Be aware that raising a litter of puppies is both time consuming and expensive, especially for Great Danes. Great Danes are capable of producing enormous litters. Expenses to raise a large brood of

Participating in sports with your Great Dane will help you strengthen your bond.

puppies can be significant. If pregnancy or birthing complications arise, you can expect to pay twice the veterinary costs for your double-sized dog. Reputable breeders are the first to admit that dog breeding, when done right, is never a money-making endeavor.

But dog fanciers are very passionate people. The thrill of the win and the challenge to produce the best of the best are well worth all the demands. To the most dedicated, dog showing is not a sport; it is a way of life. If the Great Dane breed excites you more than anything else, by all means don't let the challenges discourage you from participating in showing and breeding. The rewards go beyond a ribbon on the wall or a trophy on the shelf!

Contact a local Great Dane club and get referrals for show dog breeders. Seek out professionals who can give you expert advice in choosing your first show dog. Educate yourself by studying the Great Dane breed standard. Attend as many dog shows as possible so that you can learn how they are organized and what you can expect. Enroll your dog in conformation training classes so that you can learn how to handle your dog, and your dog can learn the manners he needs to impress the judges.

Then practice at a few "fun matches" to get your feet wet. Fun matches are informal-type shows that do not award points toward championships, but they are a valuable training ground for novice dogs and handlers. Check the AKC's website at www.akc.org for a schedule of fun shows in your area.

There is a lot to learn in this specialized sport, but a mentor can help you avoid any pitfalls. It makes an easier transition into this type of lifestyle when you can benefit from the wisdom and knowledge of someone more experienced. Your breeder may offer to take you under her wing in her desire to see one of her precious pups succeed. You can also contact your local Great Dane club to seek a mentor.

Flyball

Some Great Danes go bonkers for balls. If your dog has a fixation for fetching, you might want to consider the canine sport of flyball. This sport consists of a 51-foot (15.5-m) course with several jumps and a ball-launching box at the end. The dog must jump the obstacles to get to the box, press a lever on the box to release a ball, then carry the ball back through the course to his handler. It is an extremely fast-paced sport that is great fun for the dogs, as well as for their owners and spectators.

Flyball is a relay-type race, where each team is composed of four dogs and their handlers. The dogs take turns running the course until all of the dogs on the team have had their turn. The combined time for each team determines the winner. Teams always compete against other teams that have similar abilities, so competition is both fair and exciting. Flyball rules dictate that jump heights must be appropriate for the smallest dog on the team, so Great Danes have somewhat of an advantage in this respect.

If you are interested in giving your ball-crazy Great Dane equal amounts of fun and exercise, visit the North American Flyball Association (NAFA) website at www.flyball.com to locate a flyball club in your area. Some training is necessary to teach your dog how to negotiate the jumps and operate the ball-launching box, but if your dog is highly ball-motivated, he will pick these things up rather quickly.

Puppy Love

PUPPY PRECAUTIONS

Great Dane puppies take much longer to physically mature than smaller dogs. The Great Dane's growth plates, the area on the end of long bones where bone growth occurs, do not close until the Great Dane puppy reaches about 18 months of age. Injuries to these areas can cause permanent and debilitating damage. Take precautions to prevent injury to your Great Dane puppy as he sprouts through his phenomenal growth stages.

- You can start training your Great Dane in dog sports at a young age, but avoid obstacles and exercises that require considerable physical coordination, especially when your Great Dane is going though awkward growth spurts.
- Avoid hard running and jumping until your Great Dane is physically mature.
- Avoid playing with your puppy on slippery surfaces, either indoors or outdoors.
- Avoid exhausting your puppy, as this can contribute to clumsiness.

Obedience

Obedience training is always a worthwhile endeavor. In addition to providing opportunities to earn some impressive titles in the obedience ring, obedience training allows you to enjoy a well-trained dog at home. Competitive obedience consists of several different levels of competition so that participants can enjoy progressing to more challenging and prestigious heights.

Don't let your Great Dane be a couch potato! Even just taking him for a brisk walk is better than not giving him any opportunities to expend some energy.

At the novice level of AKC obedience trials, dogs are required to execute basic obedience commands, such as *come*, *stay*, and *heel*, as well as other skills, such as standing for examination. Dogs who successfully perform these skills in the presence of three different judges earn a Companion Dog (CD) title. Once your dog earns a title, you may use the abbreviation for the title after your dog's registered name.

The Open level requires a higher proficiency in basic obedience skills, as the dog must perform these skills off leash. It also requires additional skills, such as retrieving over jumps and out-of-sight *stays*. The dog who successfully demonstrates these skills in the presence of three different judges earns a Companion Dog Excellent (CDX) title.

The highest level of obedience competition is the Utility level. This level requires the dog to have the utmost control. In addition to showing proficiency in the skills required at the lower levels of competition, he must master scent discrimination, directed jumping, directed retrieving, and hand signals. Dogs who perform these skills adequately for three different judges earn a Utility Dog (UD) title.

Dogs who possess a UD title can continue to compete at the Open and Utility levels to acquire enough qualifying scores to obtain a Utility Dog Excellent (UDX) title. But the competition doesn't end there. Additional points acquired from Open and Utility competitions can ultimately lead to an Obedience Trial Champion (OTCH) title.

Great Danes tend to fare quite well

in the obedience ring, so if you enjoy training your dog, obedience trials are a good outlet for your passion. They are also good places to develop friendships with other dog lovers! Visit the AKC's website at www.akc.org to study the rule book that governs this sport. Then, contact training facilities in your area to enroll in obedience classes appropriate for your skill level. A quality instructor will get you started in the right direction.

Therapy Work

You and your dog don't necessarily need a competitive spirit to enjoy doing special things together. Perhaps your Great Dane really loves people, and you'd like to share his gentle, outgoing nature with others. The Great Dane's typically laid-back personality makes him an excellent candidate for therapy dog work, but this isn't the only qualification on his resume. His height makes it easy for people to pet him from a wheelchair. And his short, clean coat is especially desirable in health care institutions.

Therapy dog work has broadened to offer many different kinds of opportunities for you and your dog. You can share your dog's affection with nursing home residents, hospital patients, or schoolchildren. Your dog can assist children or adults with reading programs, grief support, or physical rehabilitation. But not every Great Dane is perfectly

suited for this kind of work, nor is every Great Dane owner. Ask yourself the following questions before deciding to undertake this type of volunteer job:

1. Is your Great Dane well versed in basic obedience, and has he learned to respect the personal space of humans?
2. Does your Great Dane have a quiet, calm temperament when put in new surroundings?
3. Does your Great Dane get along well with other animals?
4. Can you commit to making therapy dog visits at least once a week?

If you answered yes to all of these questions, therapy work may be a good option for you. To get started, you'll need to learn how to interact appropriately with the people you visit, as well as with the staff at the institution you service. You'll need to learn how to react if anyone treats your dog inappropriately. Your dog will need to learn to be tolerant of wheelchairs, rough handling, yelling, and other situations that might normally be upsetting to a dog.

This education is available through therapy-dog training classes offered through training facilities or therapy groups. You can locate a local therapy group through the Therapy Dogs International's (TDI) website at www.tdi-dog.org. This organization also certifies therapy dogs and can refer you to certification testing sites in your

SPORTS AND SAFETY

Most dog sports require your dog to be in good physical condition. Observe the following tips to help your dog avoid injuries:

- Introduce your dog to any physical sport gradually so that he can build up his physical condition. This is especially important for puppies, as physical stress in a growing dog can cause serious or permanent damage to joints, bones, and connective tissues.
- Don't allow your dog to overexert himself. Some dogs have incredibly strong drives that outmatch their physical abilities, and they may continue to push themselves to the detriment of their physical well-being. Your dog may have to rely on you to push the "off" button.
- Always be prepared for emergencies by bringing a pet first-aid kit to sporting events or practices.
- Seek veterinary attention immediately for any injuries your dog experiences. Small problems can easily become large problems if they are ignored.
- Inspect your dog's equipment for safety before practices and events. This includes sporting equipment like jumps, climbing walls, and ball launchers, as well as other canine paraphernalia, such as harnesses, collars, and leashes.
- If you are involved in an outdoor sport, be prepared for inclement weather. Your Great Dane may require a coat to protect him from a cold rain on a tracking course. It is not safe to practice or compete on wet agility equipment. When in doubt about safety, withdraw your dog from competition or practice.
- Do not heavily exercise your Great Dane one hour before or two hours after feeding time, as this can contribute to bloat.
- Do not participate in sports if your dog appears ill or lame. Make sure that your dog is physically and mentally up to the task.

area. The Delta Society also offers an excellent Pet Partners program that is worth exploring. Visit its website at www.deltasociety.org.

Tracking

Dogs have incredible noses, and it is fascinating to watch a dog use his extraordinary olfactory abilities. Your Great Dane, as a working dog, has plenty of determination and perseverance to follow a track to its conclusion. His size has nothing to do with his talent for scenting. Success depends on the training your dog receives and the skill you develop in "reading" your dog. Being able to recognize when your dog needs to slow down and re-evaluate his direction helps to keep him on the right track.

In the sport of tracking, a "tracklayer" walks out a track with several turns and leaves various types of articles, like gloves or clothing, for the dog to find. This sport does not involve competition among dogs and handlers—it is strictly a pass-or-fail test. If your dog makes it to the end of the track and finds all of the articles left by the tracklayer, he earns a tracking title.

The first level of tracking, which earns the title of Tracking Dog (TD), involves following a track that is 440 to 500 yards (402.5 to 457 m) long with three to five turns. This track is up to two hours old and has only one article at the end of it. The second level of tracking offers a Tracking Dog Excellent (TDX) title and requires a dog to follow a track that is 800 to 1,000 yards (731.5 to 914.5 m) long and up to five hours old. This track has five to seven turns and several articles to locate. People other than the tracklayer leave cross-tracks to further complicate

When traveling by car with your Great Dane, it's important to take certain safety precautions.

the track. The third and highest level of tracking competition offers a title in Variable Surface Tracking (VST). This challenging track requires the dog to track over various surfaces, such as concrete, grass, and gravel. The track is 600 to 800 yards (548.5 to 731.5 m) long and is aged up to five hours. It has four to eight changes in direction and four different types of articles for the dog to locate. A dog who masters all three levels of tracking competition automatically receives a Champion Tracker (CT) title.

Traveling With Your Great Dane

Traveling with a Great Dane might seem like a monstrous undertaking, but it's really no different from traveling with any other type of dog—except for size accommodations. Great Danes love the adventure of exploring new places, just like other dogs do. So why should you deny your Great Dane the fun of travel?

Traveling with your dog opens up a lot of opportunities for memory making. If you want to participate in dog sports, like conformation shows, obedience trials, or agility trials, you'll need to travel to get to various events. If you enjoy camping, hiking, boating, or other outdoor activities, your Great Dane would love to join you. No matter what your destination, traveling with a dog can be relatively stress-free when you are prepared.

Traveling by Car

If you are considering traveling by car, you might be concerned about how much room your gargantuan canine will consume in the vehicle. The safest way for a dog to travel is in a dog crate, but unless you have a full-sized van, a Great Dane-sized crate may not leave enough room for a driver. A canine seat belt might be a better option, as it can keep your dog safe in the event of an accident, as well as prevent your dog from moving about inside the vehicle. A metal cage-like barrier to keep your dog in the back of the vehicle is also a good choice.

Plan ahead before your excursion to prevent problems from cropping up.

Regardless of how you decide to restrain your dog in the car, a Great Dane can still be an imposing rear-view obstacle when he's sitting or standing in your vehicle. Teach your Great Dane to lie down whenever he is in the car. You'll be amazed at how little room he occupies in a reclining position—the Great Dane's size is more in his legs than in his bulk. If you require your dog to lie down whenever he is in the car, he will learn that this is the proper position for traveling.

The following tips will help you and your wayfaring friend have a safe and enjoyable trip.

Make a Travel List

This list should include all of the things you need to bring for your dog so that you won't forget anything. Besides the obvious items like food and water, dishes, collar, ID tags, and leash, this list should include toys to keep your dog busy, waste bags to clean up after your dog, medications your dog requires, and your veterinarian's number in case of an emergency. It's also a good idea to bring a current photo of your dog in case he gets lost. If you plan on camping, a first-aid kit is a must. You might even want to give your dog his own travel bag so that you can easily inventory his things and keep them organized.

Plan Ahead

Familiarize your dog with vehicle travel before hitting the open road. If your dog is not already accustomed to car travel, a few drives around town will give him a chance to become comfortable with it. Regardless of your destination, always make sure that your dog will be welcome there. Never assume that campgrounds always allow dogs (some don't). You might find that many "dog-friendly" hotels are only friendly to smaller dogs. And if you plan to visit relatives, a Great Dane can literally be a huge imposition. Always call ahead and make arrangements for your sizable sidekick. Also, make sure that your dog is up to date on vaccinations before embarking on a new adventure. Does he need any additional vaccinations to protect him against risks he may face at your destination? Is his microchip registration information current?

Keep Your Dog Comfortable

Be sure to give your dog plenty of breaks during a long car trip. He needs to stretch those long legs and get some fresh air once in a while. Offer him a drink occasionally so that he doesn't get dehydrated.

Keep Your Dog Safe

Never leave your dog unattended in a vehicle. Also, do not allow your dog to hang his head outside the car window while traveling, as this can lead to eye or ear injuries. And don't allow your dog off-leash in an unfamiliar area. No matter how well trained, dogs often become frightened and disoriented in strange surroundings. Always keep your dog on a leash while traveling.

Be a Responsible Dog Owner

Be considerate of others and clean up after your dog. Make sure that he does not disturb other vacationers. Always try to be a good canine ambassador wherever you go. When you make a good impression on others, it is sure to open more doors for dogs in the future so that we can all enjoy our pets more!

Traveling by Air

Traveling by automobile is definitely the preferred mode of travel for canines, especially for large dogs like Great Danes. Although most airlines allow small dogs to travel in the cabins of their airplanes, large dogs are not so fortunate. They must travel in a crate in the cargo

NYLABONE

hold along with the luggage. This area of the plane may not be climate-controlled, so it can become quite uncomfortable, especially on longer trips.

Unfortunately, situations may arise that require your Great Dane to travel by air, such as a cross-country move or an important dog show. If your Great Dane must travel by air, you need to request animal shipping requirements from the airline. Airlines are very particular about the size and type of animal crates they will accept on their planes. You must label the crate and provide certain documents for your dog, such as a health certificate and rabies certificate, according to the airline's requirements. Make sure that you understand all of these requirements ahead of time to avoid delays or missed flights.

If you plan to travel to a foreign country, you'll need to research the quarantine procedures and animal import regulations for your destination. What vaccinations will be required? Are there any unique health risks your dog may face at his destination? Do you need to obtain a specific health certificate? The following are a few additional tips provided for pet owners by the Air Transport Association of America (ATA):

- Make sure that your dog is healthy and fit to travel.
- Try to book a direct flight whenever possible.

Check It Out

SPORTS AND ACTIVITIES CHECKLIST

✓ Evaluate your dog's personality and talents when deciding on a dog sport or activity to pursue.

✓ Observe safety precautions when participating in dog sports.

✓ Make a travel list for your dog.

✓ Make lodging arrangement ahead of time when your dog accompanies you on trips.

✓ Get your dog accustomed to his crate, seat belt, or car barrier prior to travel.

✓ Teach your Great Dane to lie down when traveling in a vehicle.

✓ Be considerate of others when traveling with your dog.

✓ Request airline pet policies prior to air travel.

- Do not sedate your dog prior to air travel—tranquilizers can have undesirable effects on pets at higher altitudes.
- Make sure that your dog is comfortable in his crate prior to traveling.
- Offer your dog a light meal and water within four hours of air travel, but do not overfeed your dog—a full stomach is not good for traveling.

For additional information, visit the ATA's website at www.airlines.org.

Finding Pet-Friendly Lodging

Finding pet-friendly lodging is as easy as an Internet search. Many online resources are available to locate hotels, cottages, and resorts that accept pets, including www.dogfriendly.com, www.petswelcome.com, www.bringfido.com, and many others. However, never assume that "pet friendly" means "Dane friendly."

Always contact prospective hotels and resorts ahead of time to make specific arrangements for your oversized dog.

Some "pet-friendly" hotels have size limits on pets. Additional fees, damage deposits, and other policies vary among the different businesses. It never hurts to shop around and request pet policies in writing before making a commitment on lodging.

No matter who chooses the activities you enjoy together—you or your dog—there is an important life lesson to be learned whenever you enjoy time with your canine friend. The greatest reward goes beyond bond building, awards, titles, fun, or even the sense of goodness in giving to others; it is the simple joy of living, one moment at a time, with your remarkable canine.

Chapter
9

Health of Your
Great Dane

Good health is the substance of beauty. It polishes your Great Dane's glistening coat. It saturates your Great Dane's physique with power. It puts the sparkle in his eyes and the spring in his step. A good diet and regular exercise are the cornerstones of your dog's good health, but you need one more thing to create a complete, solid structure. Quality health care is the perfect complement to your dog's healthy lifestyle.

Finding a Veterinarian

The most important part of providing good health care for your Great Dane is finding a veterinarian to minister to his health needs. Although all licensed veterinarians are well educated and most of them are quite competent, they all have their individual strengths. Which strengths are the most important to you? Would you prefer a veterinarian who has experience with the unique health needs of the Great Dane breed? Do you need a veterinarian who can provide care for a variety of different pets? Would your Great Dane benefit from the expertise of a veterinarian with a specialty, like cardiology or ophthalmology?

Keep your individual needs in mind as you consider what kind of health care provider you'd like for your dog. Ask your breeder or Great Dane club members for recommendations. Ask your friends, relatives, and coworkers if they have had

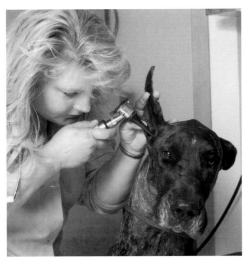

The most important part of providing good health care for your Great Dane is finding a vet to minister to his health needs.

positive experiences with any particular veterinarian. Once you've identified a good prospect, contact the veterinary hospital to continue your investigation.

You want to find out if the veterinary hospital maintains hours that are convenient for you. Can you make appointments in the evening or on weekends? Where will you have to take your dog after-hours in the case of an emergency? You should also compare prices for office charges, vaccinations, and spay or neuter surgery to make sure that they are competitive with other veterinary hospitals in your area. You can expect fees to be slightly higher at veterinary hospitals that are equipped with modern diagnostic

Ask the Expert

EXERCISE AND BLOAT

Q: Why does vigorous exercise before or after eating contribute to bloat?

A: "When a dog eats, the food can be in the stomach for one to three hours in the initial stage of digestion. Exercise at that stage can increase the accumulation of gas in the stomach due to a couple of factors. During exercise, blood is shifted to the muscles and away from the GI tract, which slows digestion. In addition, dogs may swallow air during exercise. The combination of food sitting in the stomach, more air in the stomach, and the motion of exercise can allow the stomach to start rotating and eventually flip over, causing bloat."

—LeeAnne Sherrod, D.V.M., Mukwonago Animal Hospital, Mukwonago, WI

equipment and laboratory facilities, as these amenities influence the quality of the care you can expect.

Check to see if the veterinary hospital is a member of the American Animal Hospital Association (AAHA). This organization requires its members to meet certain standards of practice and inspects them regularly. Other veterinary organizations exist to support veterinarians in various fields of specialty or alternative therapies. You can learn a lot about a veterinarian by asking if she maintains an affiliation with any professional organizations.

If the veterinary hospital appears to be a good match for your needs, it's time to evaluate the veterinarian in person. In most cases, you'll do this when you make the first veterinary appointment for your dog. This is a good time to observe the cleanliness and organization of the veterinary hospital. Does the staff treat you and your dog with respect and courtesy? Does the veterinarian explain things so that you can understand them? And finally, does she seem like someone you can trust to provide the best care possible for your beloved Great Dane?

The Veterinary Exam

Your Great Dane should receive a veterinary exam shortly after you acquire him. This is necessary to identify any health problems as soon as possible. It may also be required to fulfill any health guarantee requirements in a puppy sale contract. Puppies require several veterinary visits between the ages of 8 weeks and 16 weeks to obtain a series of puppy vaccinations. The AAHA recommends annual exams for adult dogs, and it suggests more frequent exams for senior dogs.

Be prepared for these routine veterinary exams. Write down any questions you may have concerning your dog's health or behavior so that you won't forget to ask your veterinarian about them. Bring a stool sample so that your veterinarian can check for intestinal parasites. You might want to bring a few doggy treats to ensure your dog's cooperation and to teach him that the vet's office is a good place to be. And if this is your first visit to the vet, bring along any health documentation you may have on your dog, including information on previous vaccinations, surgeries, medications, and treatments. All of these items will greatly assist your vet in delivering the best health care.

During the exam, your veterinarian will check your dog's eyes, nose, mouth, and ears for discharge or other signs of illness. She'll check your dog's heart and lungs with a stethoscope and palpate his abdomen to feel for abnormal lumps. She'll even run a finger against the lay of your dog's fur to check for signs of parasites or skin conditions. The importance of such a thorough exam cannot be understated. Dogs can't tell us when something is wrong, and they have an instinct to hide their pain. It helps to have a trained professional check for subtle signs of illness that might otherwise go unnoticed.

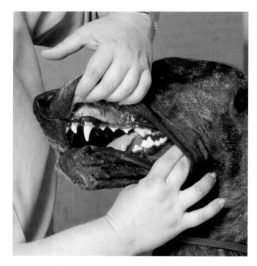
During his annual vet exam, the vet will check your dog's mouth and teeth.

Neutering and Spaying

Pet overpopulation has become a serious problem worldwide. Because of this, you should only consider breeding your Great Dane if you have a serious desire to produce top-quality dogs. If your desire is only to have a wonderful pet, there are many advantages to neutering or spaying your Great Dane.

Neutered male dogs are less likely to develop problems with roaming, marking (urinating on) furniture, and aggression. They cannot develop prostate cancer or other health problems related to the reproductive organs. Spayed female dogs cannot produce accidental litters, and they do not go through messy heat cycles

2006 CANINE VACCINE GUIDELINES

The American Animal Hospital Association's (AAHA) 2006 Canine Vaccine Guidelines recommends the following vaccine schedule for puppies:

CORE VACCINES	AGE				
	8 Weeks	12 Weeks	16 Weeks	1 Year	Over 1 Year
Distemper	X	X	X	X	3-year booster
Parvovirus	X	X	X	X	3-year booster
Canine Adenovirus-2	X	X	X	X	3-year booster
Rabies (1-year)		X		X	1-year booster
Rabies (3-year)		X		X	3-year booster
NON-CORE VACCINES	**AGE**				
	8 Weeks	12 Weeks	16 Weeks	1 Year	Over 1 Year
Parainfluenza	X	X		X	3-year booster
Bordetella	X	X			1-year booster
Leptospirosis		X	X		1-year booster

twice per year (in the case of Great Danes, the production of bloody discharge during heat cycles can be especially messy). Spayed females do not go through false pregnancies, which are a common problem for Great Danes, and they cannot suffer from uterine cancer or uterine infections. In the end, neutered and spayed dogs are simply easier to maintain.

Vaccinations

One of the things you'll want to discuss at each of your dog's veterinary exams is vaccinations. Vaccinations help protect your dog against some very dangerous diseases. "Core" vaccines are those considered necessary for all dogs, as they protect against some of the most deadly and contagious diseases. "Non-core" vaccines are those recommended on an individual basis, depending on your dog's risk of exposure.

Current AAHA canine vaccination guidelines recommend that your puppy receive a series of core vaccines between the ages of 8 and 16 weeks. He should receive a set of booster vaccinations at one year of age and every three years thereafter. Non-core vaccines may require annual or three-year boosters, depending on the vaccine. Your veterinarian can help you keep your dog up to date with his various vaccination requirements.

Dogs are often vaccinated against the following diseases.

Adenoviruses

Canine Adenovirus-1 targets the dog's liver and kidneys. It results in infectious canine hepatitis, which causes symptoms of jaundice, such as a yellowing of the dog's skin or eyes. It can also cause lethargy, fevers, and internal bleeding. Treatment may consist of intravenous fluids, broad-spectrum antibiotics to prevent secondary infections, and large doses of B Complex and B-12 vitamins. Blood transfusions may be necessary in severe cases.

Canine adenovirus-2 causes mild respiratory distress in the form of coughing. It does not usually cause serious illness unless there are other underlying health issues, but it can contribute to the condition known as kennel cough, in which case cough suppressants may be necessary to relieve symptoms.

Distemper

Distemper is a common killer of puppies and can be fatal for 50 percent of the adult dogs it ravages. Its symptoms can include discharge from the nose and eyes, lethargy, vomiting, diarrhea and fever. Treatment involves supportive care, such as IV fluids, antibiotics, and anti-diarrheal medications. Advanced cases may require sedatives and anticonvulsants to manage seizures. The dire prognosis for distemper and its highly contagious nature are good

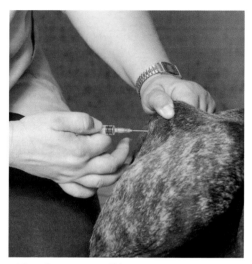

Your Great Dane will be vaccinated against a variety of diseases.

cause to classify the distemper vaccine as a core vaccine.

Kennel Cough

Kennel cough acquired its name from the dry, hacking cough it causes. Three different infectious agents are suspected of contributing to this highly contagious condition: The viruses canine adenovirus-2 and canine parainfluenza, and the bacterium *Bordetella bronchiseptica*. The bordetella vaccine is administered intranasally (sprayed into the nostrils). Although kennel cough is not serious and the vaccine is not a core vaccine, vaccination is recommended for any dog who comes in contact with a lot of other dogs. This highly contagious illness can spread through a breeding kennel, boarding kennel, dog show, or dog park very quickly. Mild cases do not usually require treatment, as the illness tends to runs its course within a few weeks. When symptoms make a dog exceptionally uncomfortable, cough suppressants may be prescribed by a veterinarian. More severe cases may require bronchodilator medications to ease breathing and antibiotics to address secondary infections.

Leptospirosis

Leptospirosis is a bacterial infection that affects a dog's liver and kidneys. It produces symptoms of jaundice, lethargy, vomiting, and fever. Treatment often consists of anti-vomiting and anti-diarrheal medications, IV fluids, and antibiotic treatments. Because the risk of infection is limited to those areas where outbreaks have occurred, it is not necessary to vaccinate the general canine population. Your veterinarian can advise you if this vaccine is a necessary precaution in your area.

Lyme Disease

Dogs acquire Lyme disease through the bite of an infected tick. The bacterium that causes Lyme disease is responsible for causing a variety of symptoms, including lameness, arthritis, swelling of the joints, loss of appetite, and

lethargy. Affected dogs usually respond to antibiotic treatment, but if you live in an area where ticks thrive, or if you do a lot of camping with your dog, the Lyme vaccine may be well worth considering.

Parainfluenza

Just like its name suggests, canine parainfluenza is a dog flu. It causes symptoms similar to human flu, including nasal discharge, coughing, congestion, and a general feeling of malaise. Supportive care may include the administration of IV fluids and antibiotics. Although most dogs recover from canine parainfluenza, it can be dangerous for the very young, the very old, or dogs with compromised immune systems. Although the parainfluenza vaccine is not a core vaccine, many veterinarians recommend it anyway, simply because the disease produces such miserable symptoms and can result in complications.

Parvovirus

Parvovirus is another serious virus that warrants vaccination for all dogs. This virus targets the gastrointestinal system and can cause bloody diarrhea, lethargy, vomiting, and fever. Like other potentially deadly viruses, it is particularly dangerous for puppies. Affected dogs are treated with IV fluids, electrolyte replacement, anti-vomiting and anti-diarrheal medications, and broad-spectrum

EAR CROPPING

Ear cropping is one procedure for which you should seek specialized veterinary care. If you are faced with the option of cropping your Great Dane's ears, be aware that ear cropping is an art that requires careful evaluation of the thickness of ear leather and the conformation of the head. Not all veterinarians are adept at this procedure. You may need to find someone other than your regular veterinarian to perform this surgery. Great Dane breeders and Great Dane club members are a good source of referrals.

There are a number of things that you should consider before deciding to crop your dog. First, understand that there are risks involved in any type of surgery that requires anesthesia. Complications may arise in the form of bleeding or infection. And of course, it is a relatively painful operation, which is why you should have it done before your dog is 12 weeks old.

Second, there is always the chance of minor imperfections. Many veterinarians will not guarantee the results of cropping simply because they cannot control the natural shrinking, wrinkling, or scarring of tissues during the healing process. There is always a chance that things will not come out quite as attractively as you had hoped.

And third, be prepared to invest in your dog's postoperative care. Depending on the length of the cropped ears and your dog's individual ear characteristics, you may need to keep your dog's ears taped in the proper position anywhere from a couple weeks to several months. Failure to do so may result in serious deformities. The trick is not to give up on this task until you achieve the proper ear set. Your veterinarian will show you how to tape your dog's ears correctly.

If you do not think that you have the patience for this kind of follow-up care, consider the natural look instead. It will give your Great Dane a softer appearance, and in some cases, this is a good thing. The Great Dane is intimidating enough in size. A softer profile makes him a little more approachable, a quality especially important for a family or therapy dog. Think about your future goals for your dog and whether your reasons for cropping justify the drawbacks.

antibiotics. Dogs who are fortunate enough to survive parvo may suffer permanent damage.

Rabies

The rabies virus causes devastating neurological symptoms in dogs, which include an inability to swallow, delirium, and vicious behavior. This disease is highly contagious and always fatal. Its potential transmission to humans makes it a very serious public health concern. For this reason, not only is the rabies vaccine a core vaccine, it is also required by law. Most communities require proof of rabies vaccination before they will issue a dog license.

Parasites

Although your Great Dane may face some health problems that are beyond your control, you'd be surprised how much influence you have on the outcome. Maintaining your dog in good health makes him resistant to disease and helps him to recover faster when health challenges beset him. You can give your dog the best chance of surviving health setbacks by being alert to symptoms of illness, providing prompt treatment for your dog, and protecting your dog from parasite infestations. Both external and internal parasites can have a serious impact on your Great Dane's general health.

External Parasites

Parasites are selfish little organisms that obtain their sustenance from a host species without contributing anything to their hosts in return. External parasites live in or on the skin of their hosts. Some of them are visible to the naked eye and some of them are not, but all of them are capable of producing very visible symptoms. The most common creatures in the "cootie" category for dogs are fleas and ticks.

Fleas

Fleas have a notorious reputation. They reproduce so rapidly that a minor flea problem can become a major one within a few short weeks. They bite their hosts to feed on blood, and they cause intense itching that makes dogs horribly miserable. Infested dogs often suffer skin damage and hair loss from scratching. Worst of all, fleas often transmit tapeworms to dogs.

If your dog seems to be scratching more than usual, check him for fleas. It's fairly easy to spot fleas in a Great Dane's short coat. You'll notice tiny dark brown bugs scurrying along your dog's skin, or you'll see tiny black flecks of "flea dirt" (flea waste) in his coat.

Your dog's trim coat makes it easier to treat for fleas, as insecticidal products can easily penetrate his fur. Many flea treatment products are on the market, but always use these products according to

Check your Great Dane for fleas and ticks after he's been playing outside.

the directions. Make sure that whatever product you use is safe for all of the different animal species that live in your home. And never use more than one insecticidal product on your dog at a time—this includes flea collars, sprays, dips, powders, and shampoos.

In addition to killing the fleas on your dog, you will also have to treat your dog's living environment. Insecticidal sprays designed for household use work well for this. Spray them on your pet's beds, along baseboards, and under furniture where fleas like to lay their eggs. If the flea problem is pervasive, an insecticidal fogger may be preferable. You may need to treat your dog and your premises more than once to get a serious flea infestation under control.

The easiest way to deal with fleas is to be proactive in preventing them. Many effective preventives are available,

including flea collars, topical treatments, and oral tablets. These are definitely worth considering, especially in warmer climates where fleas present an ongoing challenge.

Ticks

Flea preventives can also help kill and repel another bloodsucking parasite: ticks. These spider-like creatures do not cause much physical discomfort for dogs, but they are just as detrimental to your pet's health. Ticks transmit several potentially serious diseases to dogs, including Lyme disease, ehrlichiosis, tick paralysis, and Rocky Mountain spotted fever.

If you live in tick habitat, a preventive is worth the investment. Check your dog frequently during tick season in the spring and summer. Make a habit of petting your dog lightly and thoroughly every day to feel for small lumps on his skin. Ticks tend to favor a dog's neck and ears, but you may also find them on other parts of your dog's body.

The sooner you remove a tick, the less chance it will have of transmitting a disease to your pet. If you find a tick, grasp it close to the dog's skin with a tweezers and pull it off quickly. Kill the tick by immersing it in rubbing alcohol. Then disinfect the bite site to prevent infection.

Internal Parasites

Parasites are not always so easy to detect. Some parasites live inside the dog's body and cause much more subtle symptoms. Intestinal worms, like roundworms, hookworms, and whipworms, can cause a dull coat and poor skin condition. Sometimes a slightly bloated belly and a subdued energy level are the only indications of an intestinal worm infection. In many cases, though, these parasites proliferate undetected.

Puppies often acquire roundworms from their mothers, either through their mother's blood supply before birth or through their mother's milk after they are born. It's not unusual for worm larvae to become encysted in a mother dog's tissues, and in an encysted state, the worms are impervious to worming treatments. Pregnancy activates the encysted larvae, which enables them to infect the puppies.

While adult dogs can more easily tolerate a load of worms, puppies' little bodies are much more prone to the detrimental effects of parasites. The burden on their systems can make it difficult for them to grow and thrive properly. Your veterinarian can prescribe the right course of treatment for your puppy, and it is a good idea to have your adult dog's stool checked annually for parasite infection.

Tapeworms are unique among intestinal worm species in that they can grow quite long. The most common tapeworm in dogs, *Dipylidium caninum*, can grow up to 20 inches (50 cm) long. Their segmented bodies break off into confetti-sized pieces that may appear around the dog's rectum and in his stool. These segments dry into hard egg casings that release thousands of tapeworm eggs. Worming treatments for other types of intestinal worms are not effective against tapeworms, so your veterinarian will have to prescribe an appropriate tapeworm treatment. Fleas serve as intermediate hosts for tapeworms. They eat the tapeworm eggs and then transmit tapeworms to dogs. To prevent tapeworms, you must keep your dog free of fleas!

The most devastating internal parasite targets a different part of the dog's body. Heartworms travel to the cardiopulmonary system and seek out the dog's heart to

Giving your Great Dane enough exercise is crucial to his health and well-being.

A FIRST-AID KIT FOR FIDO

Dogs can suffer illnesses and injuries just like people do. Are you prepared to deal with the inevitable scrapes, bumps, bruises, or medical emergencies your Great Dane may experience? A pet first-aid kit can be especially helpful if you enjoy traveling with your Great Dane or participating in dog sports. A small toolbox or tackle box makes a wonderful first-aid supply organizer. Consider including the following items in your kit:

- *Benadryl for severe allergic reactions or severe bee stings
- *buffered aspirin for pain relief
- bandage scissors
- contact information for the nearest emergency veterinary hospital
- cotton swabs
- document of your dog's normal vital signs (pulse, respiration rate, and body temperature) for comparison purposes
- eye wash
- first-aid tape
- first-aid instruction booklet
- gauze rolls
- hotline number for the ASPCA Poison Control Center (888-426-4435)

- hydrogen peroxide
- instant heat/cold packs
- muzzle, rope, or strip of cloth
- oral syringe
- petroleum jelly
- rectal thermometer
- rubbing alcohol
- sterile gauze pads
- styptic powder or other blood coagulant agent
- triple antibiotic ointment
- tweezers for removing splinters or ticks
- vet's contact information
- vet wrap bandaging

*Obtain dosage instructions from your veterinarian

take up residence. Like other types of internal parasites, symptoms can be rather nonspecific until the infection becomes severe. When the heart's function becomes impaired, it may result in a lack of energy, coughing, or collapse. If left untreated, heartworms are fatal.

Heartworms can be difficult and risky to treat, as the veterinarian must introduce poison into the dog's system to kill the worms. This can be hard on the dog, and the dog's body must then absorb the dead worms, which can also cause complications. The best policy in dealing with these deadly parasites is prevention. Make sure that your dog receives regular heartworm tests and heartworm preventives.

Common Hereditary Conditions

Many health conditions faced by dogs have a hereditary link. In the case of purebred dogs, the chance of a dog acquiring a heritable disorder depends on the amount of inbreeding in his history and whether his sire and dam have been tested and cleared of carrying defective genes. Regardless of how well bred your Great Dane may be, you should be aware of the common hereditary conditions that manifest in this breed and be able to recognize the symptoms.

Bloat

Bloat is a common problem for many large, deep-chested breeds like the Great Dane. There are actually two separate conditions associated with bloat. Gastric dilatation occurs when the dog's stomach becomes bloated and distended from overeating or consuming inappropriate things, like yeast, that cause gas to build up in the stomach. A veterinarian can treat this condition by passing a tube

down the dog's throat to the stomach to relieve the stomach pressure. It is often necessary to induce the dog to vomit to empty the stomach's contents.

When the bloated stomach twists within the abdomen and pinches off its entry and exit points, gastric dilatation-volvulus (GDV) has occurred. Both of these conditions are very serious and can kill a dog in a short period. In the case of GVD, a tube cannot pass into the stomach, so the veterinarian may have to penetrate the abdomen with a needle to relieve stomach pressure. Immediate surgery is required to rotate the stomach back to its normal position, and the stomach is sutured in place to prevent a recurrence.

The symptoms of bloat are quite obvious, as it is an extremely painful condition. Signs of discomfort include whining, biting at the abdomen, restlessness, and pacing. Affected dogs may drool or attempt to vomit or defecate without success. Their stomachs may be visually bloated or feel hard to the touch. These are all signs of a medical emergency.

It is important for Great Dane owners to manage their dogs in ways that prevent bloat. Be sure to feed your dog two smaller meals per day rather than one large one. Avoid exercising your dog within one hour before or two hours after feeding. And take precautions to prevent your dog from overeating or consuming inappropriate items.

Bloat is a common problem for large, deep-chested breeds like the Great Dane.

Endocrine Disorders

The endocrine system performs an amazing balancing act as it regulates hormone levels throughout the body. Hormones affect the function of many organs within the body, and when the endocrine system doesn't work properly, all kinds of internal mayhem can occur.

Both Addison's disease and hypothyroidism are considered autoimmune diseases. They occur when the dog's own immune system attacks and destroys the hormone-producing glands and leaves their function impaired. Damaged glands are irreparable, and affected dogs must receive hormone supplements for the duration of their lives.

Addison's Disease

The Great Dane occasionally suffers from Addison's disease, which is caused when the adrenal glands produce an insufficient amount of corticosteroids and cortisol.

Symptoms of Addison's disease include vomiting, diarrhea, and lethargy. Because these symptoms are similar to those of other illnesses, a blood test is necessary to accurately diagnose Addison's disease. Treatment consists of replacing the missing hormones with supplements. Although the prognosis for treated dogs is good, treatment is quite expensive, especially for a large dog like the Great Dane.

Hypothyroidism

Hypothyroidism is another endocrine disorder that affects Great Danes. When the thyroid gland fails to produce enough hormones to regulate the dog's metabolism, symptoms of patchy hair loss, weight gain, and intolerance to cold temperatures may occur. Diagnosis is confirmed with a blood test, and treatment consists of hormone supplements that are, thankfully, quite inexpensive.

Heart Disease

The most common type of heart disease that affects Great Danes is dilated cardiomyopathy (DCM). This condition causes an enlarged heart, particularly with regard to the left ventricle. An enlarged heart cannot operate efficiently and will cause symptoms that include a loss of coordination, lack of energy, abnormally heavy breathing with activity, and coughing during exercise.

This is a progressive disease that, unfortunately, often reaches a critical stage by the time symptoms become obvious. There is no cure, but medications may help improve the dog's quality of life and slow the disease's progression. The dire outcome of this disease is a good reason to ask breeders if their breeding stock receives regular (every two years) echocardiograms before you purchase a puppy. If your Great Dane shows symptoms of heart disease, your veterinarian may recommend an echocardiogram, an electrocardiogram, or an X-ray of your dog's chest to confirm a diagnosis.

If your dog seems unusually lethargic or generally unwell, take him to the vet.

Growth Disorders

Great Danes grow so rapidly during their first year of life that sometimes their bones grow at a rate disproportionate to the growth of surrounding tissues. A condition called eosinophilic panosteitis results when tendons and ligaments become inflamed and acutely painful. Your young Great Dane may indicate his discomfort by whimpering, limping, or acting reluctant to move.

Your veterinarian may recommend a special diet to restrict calories and therefore slow down growth until this uncomfortable growth stage passes. You can take other steps to keep your dog comfortable as well. Keep exercise to a minimum to avoid contributing to the inflammation, and give your dog a comfortable place to recline. Your veterinarian can prescribe pain medication if pain is severe. With proper dietary management, this condition eventually resolves itself.

Hip Dysplasia

Hip dysplasia is a very common problem for many large dogs. This involves a malformed hip joint that doesn't provide a secure seat for the end of the femur (thigh) bone. This eventually causes the hip joint to deteriorate with wear, resulting in pain and sometimes disability for the dog. The most obvious symptoms are lameness and an abnormal gait.

The severity of this condition depends on the extent of the joint deformity. Some dogs live good-quality lives with exercise restrictions and pain management. Others require surgery to restore a functioning joint. Responsible breeders obtain hip X-rays of their breeding stock and register the results with the Orthopedic Foundation for Animals (OFA).

Wobblers Syndrome

Wobblers syndrome earned its name from the wobbly appearance of affected dogs. This condition consists of unstable neck vertebrae that put pressure on the spinal cord and cause the dog to lose some coordination. It can be very painful for the dog and cause him to walk with his head lowered. He may yip in pain when ascending or descending stairs or show other signs of discomfort.

Like hip dysplasia, the severity of this disease varies from one case to another. Some dogs live full lives and experience minimal problems with this defect. Others degenerate until they become incapacitated. Surgery for this condition is both risky and expensive, so it is not always a practical option. Milder cases often respond well to anti-inflammatory medications and alternative therapies.

Alternative Therapies

Health care for pets has progressed to a level comparable to that available for humans, with more diagnostic and treatment options available than ever before. But conventional veterinary medicine is not the only area of pet health that has advanced. Alternative therapies, like herbal treatments, homeopathy, chiropractic, and acupuncture, have become more readily available to help our furry friends.

Veterinary specialties now exist in each of these fields so that they can effectively and safely supplement conventional medical treatments. Alternative therapies are a good consideration when synthetic medications are ineffective or produce undesirable side effects. They can also help facilitate healing and aid in rapid recoveries from surgery or illness. They can become a regular part of your dog's preventive health maintenance routine. Sometimes they can even help with behavioral issues.

Always seek out a veterinary specialist for your alternative therapy needs. The Veterinary Botanical Medicine Association (VBMA) certifies veterinarians in herbal medicine and provides a directory of its members at its website, www.vbma.org. The Academy of Veterinary Homeopathy (AVH) provides a member list and valuable information about this specialty at its website, www. theavh.org. Animal chiropractors can be located through the American Veterinary Chiropractic Association (AVCA) website

Great Danes can suffer from hip dysplasia, a condition in which a malformed hip joint doesn't provide a secure seat for the end of the femur.

at www.animalchiropractic.org. For more information or veterinary referrals for acupuncture specialists, consult the American Academy of Veterinary Acupuncture (AAVA) website at www. aava.org.

Senior Dogs

There is no doubt that modern veterinary medicine is helping our pets live longer, healthier lives. This is great news for Great Danes, who tend to get the short end of the stick when it comes to canine longevity. Because Great Danes have an average life span of seven to ten years, you want to do what you can to help your Great Dane reach the high end of that range. In fact, it's not so unusual these days for a Great Dane to reach 11 years of age with proper care and management.

Health Problems Related to Aging

Your Great Dane may start showing signs of age when he reaches about six years of age. He'll sleep more. His wild romps will become tamer. As you begin to enjoy your dog's mellowing personality, you might also notice some physical changes in him. Maybe he doesn't see or hear as well as he used to. Maybe he moves a little more stiffly.

Dogs are amazingly adaptable and often adjust to such age-related changes with grace. Still, you can help your dog weather some of the inevitable effects of aging. If his vision has diminished, avoid rearranging your furniture. If your dog has difficulty hearing, use hand signs more often to communicate with him. And if he suffers from arthritis, offer him an orthopedic or heated bed in a draft-free area.

Your old friend deserves a few comforts at this age. He also deserves a little extra veterinary attention. Never assume that the physical changes you see in your senior dog are untreatable. Vision loss may be due to cataracts or other treatable eye conditions. Hearing loss may be due

to a serious ear infection. And severe arthritis can be relieved with dietary supplements and pain medications. Other age-related conditions, such as urinary incontinence, digestive upsets, and organ failure often respond well to medications or special diets. Always address your dog's age-related conditions with your veterinarian.

Affording your dog the best quality of life in his golden years is a small price to pay for the richness with which he has painted your life.

Diet and Exercise

You cannot stop the aging process, but there are ways to slow it down. Your Great

Your Great Dane may start showing signs of age when he reaches about six years of age.

Check It Out

HEALTH CHECKLIST

✓ Consider your specific needs when choosing a veterinarian.

✓ Obtain the appropriate series of vaccinations for your Great Dane puppy.

✓ Schedule your adult Great Dane for annual veterinary exams.

✓ Use flea, tick, and heartworm preventives to keep your dog healthy.

✓ Learn to recognize the symptoms of heritable disorders so that you can provide prompt treatment for your dog.

✓ Monitor your dog's weight and adjust his food intake as he gets older.

✓ Discuss any age-related conditions with your veterinarian.

Dane's lifestyle, in the form of diet and exercise, has a huge impact on his senior health and longevity. This is the point in your dog's life when the quality diet and regular exercise you have provided your dog throughout his life begin to pay dividends. It is also a time to re-evaluate his diet and exercise needs.

Your dog has entered a new life stage. He isn't as active as he used to be, and he doesn't burn as many calories as he used to. In addition, his metabolism may become sluggish due to the lower levels of hormones his body produces. All of this adds up to the fact that your dog doesn't need to consume as much food as he used to. Check his weight frequently to make sure that he isn't gaining too much weight, as obesity is just as much a problem for older dogs as it is for older people.

Your dog's exercise needs may have diminished as well, but it's still vitally important to exercise him regularly. Moderation is the key to avoid straining older muscles and joints. A daily walk should be sufficient to keep your dog's joints flexible and his muscles toned. A little playtime is good for his mental and physical health as well. You can enjoy spending time with your dog no matter his age!

Through every stage of his life, the indomitable Great Dane is worthy of our awe and adoration. For every ounce of respect we give him, he gives us a pound of fidelity in return. And in the end, we are left with a sizeable inheritance—that which can only be granted by the preeminent "king of dogs."

Resources

Associations and Organizations

Breed Clubs

American Kennel Club (AKC)
5580 Centerview Drive
Raleigh, NC 27606
Telephone: (919) 233-9767
Fax: (919) 233-3627
E-Mail: info@akc.org
www.akc.org

Canadian Kennel Club (CKC)
89 Skyway Avenue, Suite 100
Etobicoke, Ontario M9W 6R4
Telephone: (416) 675-5511
Fax: (416) 675-6506
E-Mail: information@ckc.ca
www.ckc.ca

Federation Cynologique Internationale (FCI)
Secretariat General de la FCI
Place Albert 1er, 13
B – 6530 Thuin
Belqique
www.fci.be

Great Dane Club of America
www.gdca.org

The Great Dane Club of Canada
www.gdcc.ca

The Kennel Club
1 Clarges Street
London
W1J 8AB
Telephone: 0870 606 6750
Fax: 0207 518 1058
www.the-kennel-club.org.uk

United Kennel Club (UKC)
100 E. Kilgore Road
Kalamazoo, MI 49002-5584
Telephone: (269) 343-9020
Fax: (269) 343-7037
E-Mail: pbickell@ukcdogs.com
www.ukcdogs.com

Pet Sitters

National Association of Professional Pet Sitters
15000 Commerce Parkway, Suite C
Mt. Laurel, New Jersey 08054
Telephone: (856) 439-0324
Fax: (856) 439-0525
E-Mail: napps@ahint.com
www.petsitters.org

Pet Sitters International
201 East King Street
King, NC 27021-9161
Telephone: (336) 983-9222
Fax: (336) 983-5266
E-Mail: info@petsit.com
www.petsit.com

Rescue Organizations and Animal Welfare Groups

American Humane Association (AHA)

63 Inverness Drive East
Englewood, CO 80112
Telephone: (303) 792-9900
Fax: 792-5333
www.americanhumane.org

American Society for the Prevention of Cruelty to Animals (ASPCA)

424 E. 92nd Street
New York, NY 10128-6804
Telephone: (212) 876-7700
www.aspca.org

The Humane Society of the United States (HSUS)

2100 L Street, NW
Washington DC 20037
Telephone: (202) 452-1100
www.hsus.org

Royal Society for the Prevention of Cruelty to Animals (RSPCA)

RSPCA Enquiries Service
Wilberforce Way, Southwater,
Horsham, West Sussex RH13 9RS
United Kingdom
Telephone: 0870 3335 999
Fax: 0870 7530 284
www.rspca.org.uk

Sports

International Agility Link (IAL)

Global Administrator: Steve Drinkwater
E-Mail: yunde@powerup.au
www.agilityclick.com/~ial

The World Canine Freestyle Organization, Inc.

P.O. Box 350122
Brooklyn, NY 11235
Telephone: (718) 332-8336
Fax: (718) 646-2686
E-Mail: WCFODOGS@aol.com
www.worldcaninefreestyle.org

Therapy

Delta Society

875 124th Ave, NE, Suite 101
Bellevue, WA 98005
Telephone: (425) 679-5500
Fax: (425) 679-5539
E-Mail: info@DeltaSociety.org
www.deltasociety.org

Therapy Dogs Inc.

P.O. Box 20227
Cheyenne WY 82003
Telephone: (877) 843-7364
Fax: (307) 638-2079
E-Mail: therapydogsinc@qwestoffice.net
www.therapydogs.com

Therapy Dogs International (TDI)

88 Bartley Road
Flanders, NJ 07836

Telephone: (973) 252-9800
Fax: (973) 252-7171
E-Mail: tdi@gti.net
www.tdi-dog.org

Training

Association of Pet Dog Trainers (APDT)

150 Executive Center Drive Box 35
Greenville, SC 29615
Telephone: (800) PET-DOGS
Fax: (864) 331-0767
E-Mail: information@apdt.com
www.apdt.com

International Association of Animal Behavior Consultants (IAABC)

565 Callery Road
Cranberry Township, PA 16066
E-Mail: info@iaabc.org
www.iaabc.org

National Association of Dog Obedience Instructors (NADOI)

PMB 369
729 Grapevine Hwy.
Hurst, TX 76054-2085
www.nadoi.org

Veterinary and Health Resources

Academy of Veterinary Homeopathy (AVH)

P.O. Box 9280
Wilmington, DE 19809
Telephone: (866) 652-1590
Fax: (866) 652-1590
www.theavh.org

American Academy of Veterinary Acupuncture (AAVA)

P.O. Box 1058
Glastonbury, CT 06033
Telephone: (860) 632-9911
Fax: (860) 659-8772
www.aava.org

American Animal Hospital Association (AAHA)

12575 W. Bayaud Ave.
Lakewood, CO 80228
Telephone: (303) 986-2800
Fax: (303) 986-1700
E-Mail: info@aahanet.org
www.aahanet.org/index.cfm

American College of Veterinary Internal Medicine (ACVIM)

1997 Wadsworth Blvd., Suite A
Lakewood, CO 80214-5293
Telephone: (800) 245-9081
Fax: (303) 231-0880
Email: ACVIM@ACVIM.org
www.acvim.org

American College of Veterinary Ophthalmologists (ACVO)
P.O. Box 1311
Meridian, ID 83860
Telephone: (208) 466-7624
Fax: (208) 466-7693
E-Mail: office09@acvo.com
www.acvo.com

American Holistic Veterinary Medical Association (AHVMA)
2218 Old Emmorton Road
Bel Air, MD 21015
Telephone: (410) 569-0795
Fax: (410) 569-2346
E-Mail: office@ahvma.org
www.ahvma.org

American Veterinary Medical Association (AVMA)
1931 North Meacham Road, Suite 100
Schaumburg, IL 60173-4360
Telephone: (847) 925-8070
Fax: (847) 925-1329
E-Mail: avmainfo@avma.org
www.avma.org

ASPCA Animal Poison Control Center
Telephone: (888) 426-4435
www.aspca.org

British Veterinary Association (BVA)
7 Mansfield Street
London
W1G 9NQ
Telephone: 0207 636 6541
Fax: 0207 908 6349
E-Mail: bvahq@bva.co.uk
www.bva.co.uk

Canine Eye Registration Foundation (CERF)
VMDB/CERF
1717 Philo Rd
P O Box 3007
Urbana, IL 61803-3007
Telephone: (217) 693-4800
Fax: (217) 693-4801
E-Mail: CERF@vmbd.org
www.vmdb.org

Orthopedic Foundation for Animals (OFA)
2300 NE Nifong Blvd
Columbus, Missouri 65201-3856
Telephone: (573) 442-0418
Fax: (573) 875-5073
Email: ofa@offa.org
www.offa.org

US Food and Drug Administration Center for Veterinary Medicine (CVM)
7519 Standish Place
HFV-12
Rockville, MD 20855-0001
Telephone: (240) 276-9300 or (888) INFO-FDA
http://www.fda.gov/cvm

Publications
Books

Anderson, Teoti. *The Super Simple Guide to Housetraining*. Neptune City: TFH Publications, 2004.

Anne, Jonna, with Mary Straus. *The Healthy Dog Cookbook: 50 Nutritious and Delicious Recipes Your Dog Will Love*. UK: Ivy Press Limited, 2008.

Dainty, Suellen. *50 Games to Play With Your Dog*. UK: Ivy Press Limited, 2007.

Morgan, Diane. *Good Dogkeeping*. Neptune City: TFH Publications, 2005.

Magazines
AKC Family Dog
American Kennel Club
260 Madison Avenue
New York, NY 10016
Telephone: (800) 490-5675
E-Mail: familydog@akc.org
www.akc.org/pubs/familydog

AKC Gazette
American Kennel Club
260 Madison Avenue
New York, NY 10016
Telephone: (800) 533-7323
E-Mail: gazette@akc.org
www.akc.org/pubs/gazette

Dog & Kennel
Pet Publishing, Inc.
7-L Dundas Circle
Greensboro, NC 27407
Telephone: (336) 292-4272
Fax: (336) 292-4272
E-Mail: info@petpublishing.com
www.dogandkennel.com

Dogs Monthly
Ascot House
High Street, Ascot,
Berkshire SL5 7JG
United Kingdom
Telephone: 0870 730 8433
Fax: 0870 730 8431
E-Mail: admin@rtc-associates.freeserve.co.uk
www.corsini.co.uk/dogsmonthly

Websites
Nylabone
www.nylabone.com

TFH Publications, Inc.
www.tfh.com

Index

Dedication

To my husband John, who always supports me, and my beloved Angel, who introduced me to the magical world of giant dogs.

Acknowledgments

My sincere thanks to those who helped enrich this book with their expert advice and perspectives: LeeAnne Sherrod, D.V.M.; Jolene Tikalsky, President of the Great Dane Club of Milwaukee; Randy Weaver of Bluegrass Great Dane Rescue; Carol Lea Benjamin, author and dog trainer; Susan H. Smith, President of Pet Travel, Inc; and Laura M. Rubin, Rocky Mountain Rescue, Inc.

About the Author

Janice Biniok is a member of the Dog Writers Association of America (DWAA) and has written numerous books and articles on companion animals. She first became enchanted by Great Danes in 1993 after acquiring her beloved companion, Angel, who opened her eyes to the joys of big dog ownership. Janice lives on a small farm in Waukesha, Wisconsin, with her husband and two sons. For more information, visit her website at www. TheAnimalPen.com.

Photo Credits

Utekhina Anna (Shutterstock): 11; Yuri Arcurs (Shutterstock): 95; Simone van den Berg (Shutterstock): 86; Joy Brown (Shutterstock): 4, 16; Denise Campione (Shutterstock): 63; Karla Caspari (Shutterstock): front cover, spine, 12; Lars Christensen (Shutterstock): 18, 28, 65, 69, 76; epromocja (Shutterstock): 56, 84, 89; Joe Gough (Shutterstock): 42; Maria Hetting (Shutterstock): 78; Dee Hunter (Shutterstock): 21; Eric Isselée (Shutterstock): 1, 20, 23, 37, 60, 62, 68, 82, 112; Rey Kamensky (Shutterstock): 58, 71, 129; Crystal Kirk (Shutterstock): 32; Theresa Martinez (Shutterstock): 100; Quicksnap Photo (Shutterstock): 73; pixshots (Shutterstock): 25; Shutterstock: 7, 30, 39, 46, 47, 52, 66, 72, 77, 81, 98, 132; Birgit Sommer (Shutterstock): back cover, 96; Tish1 (Shutterstock): 6, 14, 27; Tootles (Shutterstock): 33; H. Tuller (Shutterstock): 35; Tund (Shutterstock): 9; April Turner (Shutterstock): 44; velora (Shutterstock): 49, 53; All other photos courtesy of Isabelle Francais and TFH archives

NATURAL with added VITAMINS
Nutri Dent ®
MD
Promotes Optimal Dental Health!

Visit
nylabone.com
Join Club NYLA
for coupons &
product
information

Dogs L♥ve 'em! ™
AVAILABLE IN MULTIPLE SIZES AND FLAVORS.

Nylabone ®
Trusted For Over 40 Years

MADE IN THE USA

Our Mission with Nutri Dent® is to promote optimal dental health for dogs through a trusted, natural, delicious chew that provides effective cleaning action...GUARANTEED to make your dog go wild with anticipation and happiness!!!

Nylabone Products • P.O. Box 427, Neptune, NJ 07754-0427 • 1-800-631-2188 • Fax: 732-988-5466
www.nylabone.com • info@nylabone.com • For more information contact your sales representative or contact us at sales@tfh.com

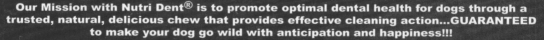